A volume in the Hyperion reprint series
THE RADICAL TRADITION IN AMERICA

LEAVES OF LIFE

A STORY OF TWENTY YEARS OF SOCIALIST AGITATION

BY J. A WAYLAND

HYPERION PRESS, INC.
Westport, Connecticut

Published in 1912 by Appeal to Reason, Girard, Kansas
Copyright 1912 by Appeal to Reason
Hyperion reprint edition 1975
Library of Congress Catalog Number 75-350
ISBN 0-88355-253-1
Printed in the United States of America

Library of Congress Cataloging in Publication Data

Wayland, Julius Augustus, 1854-1912.
   Leaves of life.

   (The Radical tradition in America)
   Reprint of the ed. published by Appeal to reason, Girard, Kan.
   1. Socialism. 2. Wayland, Julius Augustus, 1854-1912. I. Title.
HX84.W4A34   1975   335'.0092'4   75-350
ISBN 0-88355-253-1

PREFACE.

The biographies of men are usually written after they have passed from the scenes of human action, and when their lives may be passed in review by the biographer.

This little book has been prepared, not for the general public, but for that wide circle of friends that J. A. Wayland has made in the course of his remarkable newspaper career.

In 1893, Wayland began the publication of the *Coming Nation* at Greensburg, Indiana. After attaining for it a circulation of 65,000 he turned it over at Ruskin, Tenn., to the members of a colony he had organized. He went to Kansas City, Mo., and with the *Appeal to Reason* began at the bottom again. He has been connected with the *Appeal to Reason* as owner and manager for sixteen years, and it has now attained a circulation of one-half million.

During the later years of his life he has laid aside the responsibility of management, but there was a time when he was his own editor, foreman and business manager. It was during these days when few American people knew anything about Socialism that he wrote his best paragraphs and put in easy phrases the lessons of the socialist philosophy.

What Eugene V. Debs has been on the rostrum swaying vast audiences with his eloquence in a thousand cities, Wayland has been with his pen writing the thoughts that have moulded the opinions of millions.

Wayland has never sought the limelight. He has never craved publicity. He has eccentricities,—all have, and most of all great men,—but I think he is as free from vanity as any man who has ever lived. It has been his message, not himself, that he has put to the forefront always.

The *Coming Nation* was his first love. To it he gave his greatest work and enthusiasm. Think what it must have meant to him to have turned over his paper that had grown to be such a power, and see it fall into the hands of incompetents, its decay and death inevitable.

When he began again at Kansas City, what to call his new paper gave him much concern. The fact that his name was known prompted him to call it Wayland's Weekly. It was T. E. Palmer of Kansas City, an old socialist worker, who suggested the name *"Appeal to Reason,"* but it was an old German socialist in the same city who settled the question by saying: "Don't call it Wayland's Weekly, but give it a name that in time will be better known than the man who made it." This settled it,—the new paper became the "Little Old Appeal" as it is called by its friends.

Knowing Wayland as I do,—I know he would not sanction the use of laudatory language in this book, or filling it with personal encomiums, so nothing of the kind appears.

Years ago Wayland caught a vision of "a more orderly and precise state of society than that which now exists," a society where want, poverty and misery had ceased to be.

This took such hold on him that he dedicated his life to imparting it to others, for, the vision cannot materialize until society of its own free will adopts it as its own.

To the work of making others see what he had seen, he has given his unswerving devotion, and the best years of a hard worked life.

How it all happened is what I have to tell in the biographical sketch that follows.

It is told without flourish or embellishment. For the rest of the book, it contains some of the gems from Wayland's pen that have helped to make you a socialist.

The book is not for sale at any price and will be given only to the Appeal Army workers, the ones who most of all will appreciate it, and in a way with which they are familiar. A great many of you are as old as Wayland, and unless you get this book now, you may never be able to read a biography every line of which will interest you. The author of these lines was a subscriber to the old *Coming Nation* and began to take the *Appeal* when it was first started. In 1903 he was called to be a part of the editorial staff of the paper, that had made him a socialist. To the best of his knowledge his name has never been off the subscription rolls of the *Appeal,* and he accounts it as the highest honor to which he will ever attain, in having been a part of the *Appeal to*

Reason, which, perhaps more than all other educational agencies, has been instrumental in producing the social revolution in America. The preparation of this little volume has been deeply interesting. It has taken me through the files of the papers covering a period of 18 years of the storm and stress of the conflict, and has revived many forgotten incidents of the journey so many of us have traveled together.

A. W. RICKER.

Girard, Kans., Dec. 19, 1911.

J. A. WAYLAND

BIOGRAPHICAL.

Julius Augustus Wayland was born in Versailles, Indiana, April 26, 1854. His parents moved to Indiana from Kentucky when they were young. They were of Virginian stock. There were seven children—four of whom and the father were swept off in the scourge of cholera that visited Indiana in August of 1854. At the time of his death, the father was a well-to-do grocer, but owing to the illiteracy of the mother, the administrator squandered all the estate except a little four-room house, which was the saving thing between absolute pauperism and the helpless family. J. A. was the youngest, a sister of five and a brother ten years older, who are still living, being the family. Then began one of those "short and simple annals of the poor," the struggle for existence. The mother sewed, washed and worked, but kept the family together. She never married again.

Wayland says that his first impressions in childhood were the struggles to live, for the family suffered extreme poverty, especially during the war, in which the older brother enlisted. He says he remembers one winter, after they killed a pig and had a barrel of potatoes and some meal, that his mother said: "Now we will not starve this winter." He attended the village school, but when old enough to do chores, lost much of the time in the effort to earn a few cents to keep the wolf from the door. His total school days were less than two years, and most of this was spent on arithmetic and geography, in which he took great delight, and soon was ahead of his teacher. But he saw no use in grammar, and says that in after years, when he began to write for his local paper that he did not know a noun from a verb.

He did odd jobs around town and remembers that his first $5 was earned baling shingles. His ambition at this time was to be a carpenter but he could not get work. Finally he secured a job in a printing office and this was the first step in the beginning of a remarkable career. Sometime ago he wrote down some of the incidents in his life for his children, in the event of his death. In his simple way he tells this story far better than I could do it, so from this time on to the starting of the *Coming Nation* this autobiography will fill in the gap.

Home of the Coming Nation, Greensburg, Ind., 1893.

"The picture on the opposite page is the Masonic building in the court yard at Versailles, Ind., where the *Versailles Gazette* was published and in which office and building I first started to 'devil' in the printing business on April 10th, 1870; John B. Rebuck was the proprietor. I engaged to work six months for the sum of $2 per week. I had been 'rolling,' as it was then called, with the old hand presses, in the office for a year or so, but could get no steady employment, as it employed but one printer, Mr. H. M. Thompson, except on the days the paper was printed; when it required a roller boy. I didn't so much care for the wages, only I had to have enough to keep myself and mother, and we lived on this $2 a week during the six months. I wanted to learn the trade and I had pictured to myself an ideal office when I had learned enough to run one. My ideal was limited, as I had never seen any other office. This shop had a few fonts of wornout type and an old Washington hand press. That was practically the whole thing.

"After my term of apprenticeship was out I had become a good compositor and could set up any bills or ads that came into the office, but to accomplish this in so short a time I had to induce the printer to go fishing and hunting and leave me the work to do, that I might get the experience, which I knew could only come from practice, and as he could easily set all the type and do all the work without my aid, I would have gotten but little practice had he worked all the time. When the apprenticeship was out, Thompson, who got $7 a week and that very irregularly paid, concluded that he would take a rest, so I undertook to run the paper. I calculated that as Thompson had been paid $7 and myself two, that the work was worth $9 per week. My boss made no arrangement with me for wages and when I demanded that he pay the balance due me, he said he would not pay me $9 a week, but I knew he would have to, so I made him pay it and lost my job, of course. I think I had about $100 saved up when I lost my job.

"Not being able to get employment in the village, I worked in a printing office in Lawrenceburg, Ind., about thirty miles from home. Here I got additional experience. When I first saw the old country cylinder press used there I thought sure it was the biggest thing that was ever made. I wanted to run it, but I stuck to what I could do, and never asked the boss how much he was going to pay me. The foreman seemed to think I might supersede him, and to scare me away, told me that it was not likely that I would ever get all the wages coming to me as the boss was rather loose in his morals. This scared me and for an excuse to settle up I told him I was going to Cincinnati to work. He asked me what I thought I should have. I was away from home and not half so bold as in the other case, and I told him to pay me what he thought I was worth. He asked me if $10 a week was enough and I was more than surprised at the amount. I had not thought of getting over $7 though I paid $4 for board. He told me he was very sorry I was going to leave; that he liked me very much; that if I should want another job I should come back. I was sorry I told him I was going to leave, when he paid me down; but I felt ashamed to say that I would stay when I had told him I was going to leave. I then went to Cincinnati but was too bashful to ask for a job in a printing office, though I was a much better printer than the majority, but I didn't know it. I don't know what prompted me but I asked for a job on a steamboat and got it. It was the first job I had asked for, though I had been there for some weeks, stopping with an uncle. I made several trips up and down the Ohio as far as Memphis. This was in the spring of 1872. When the peach trees began to bloom I felt homesick and on the return of the boat to Cincinnati about the first of June I quit and went back to Versailles. There was nothing doing in the line of work, so I got busy on my own hook. I induced Thompson to agree to go in with me and publish a paper ourselves. Having got him worked up to this point, I went to the owner of the paper and wanted to buy it, but he did not want to sell. I told him that Thompson and I intended to start a paper, and, as we were both printers, we could do it cheaper than he could and that it would surely affect his paper. He was not a printer. Thompson did the work and wrote all the local matter, while the owner was studying law, using the paper as a means of sustaining himself during his preparation for the bar. With this view of the case, not knòwing how much money we had for our venture, he agreed to sell us the printing office for $690. Its material was worth about two hundred, but it had a great value in our eyes. I had $198 and Thompson had an unpaid labor bill against the owner of $129. This wasn't enough, but I was fertile in planning. Thompson left everything with me to arrange, he being of a very retiring disposition. I went to the newly elected county auditor, and sheriff, who were Republicans, and told them that Thompson and I had arranged to buy the *Gazette* and that we were short $350 and asked if they would not go our security for the amount. As both had patronage that could protect them in the repayment of such a sum, they agreed to endorse our notes, which they did. When we met to complete the deal, I flashed the note as a part payment. The owner saw our hand then and refused to accept that as cash. I told him all right I could easily go out and get Uncle Tom Smith, a money loaner, to cash it, and that the sheriff and auditor would give us the patronage anyhow, if he did not, and then he accepted it and closed the deal. The little money I had was saved up in small pieces of silver, very few bills being among it. We were twenty-three dollars short of the full amount, but Rebuck said he would wait a few days for that, if we would not charge him anything for getting out the next issue of the paper and give him the benefit of its business. To this we agreed and paid him over every cent we had. This was on Feb. 6, 1873, and on Feb. 13th we issued our first paper.

"We changed the name of the paper from the *Gazette* to the *'Ripley Index.'* The regular issue of the paper had been seventeen quires—408 papers—ever since I had worked in the shop. Names were never taken off except by peremptory demand, and few ever added. Some of its advertisements had run in the paper for ten years without the change of a letter. My little experience in Lawrenceburg had given me some new ideas and we proceeded to apply them. We tore down the entire paper and reset every advertisement. We made a spicy local sheet the first issue, for we had each saved up every item of news that we thought of for the whole month we were dickering on the trade. In this issue we announced that all who were in arrears for the paper would be cut off the list. But this gag had been worked so often on the readers that they paid no more attention to it than they did any other thing in the paper, which was mighty little, and, I think now, that not one in a dozen ever read it or anything else in the paper. But the management devolved on me, though the younger, and I knew we could not buy the paper and give it out on credit, so making virtue of a necessity, I determined not to send the paper to any one on credit. Some of the subscribers were ten years in arrears. To get out our first issue we had not a sheet of paper in the office, not five cents between us, but we got the retiring owner to endorse for us to the extent of one bundle of paper from the paper house in Cincinnati. When the paper came by express we had not even the money to pay the hack man for hauling it down five miles from the railroad station, to say nothing of the express! But the old man carried the account for us—in fact there was nothing else for him to do. When we got out the second issue we found we had just 72 names on the list paid in advance, and so we printed just four quires of paper for the edition! It looked mighty small—and it was, but I figured that if we didn't use the paper we would have less expense. I remember well that the morning after we had printed and put them in the office a farmer named Thomas Boswell came into the office and said his paper was not in the postoffice. I looked over the list (I knew his name had been cut off) and after meditating a minute told him that his time was out. He said that could not be for his time never ran out, as he had taken the paper for twenty years and never missed a copy. But I told him we had to have the money in advance as we had no money to buy paper with. He paid us $1.50 for a year's subscription and we were flush! We paid the hack driver and the express bill and felt that things were coming our way. Two weeks' work for two printers and the receipts were just $1.50! But my plan of advance payment was a success, and we soon had money to pay our bills, though the panic that struck the country in April of that memorable year, made it pretty hard sledding to keep our heads above the wreck and ruin that bestrewed the country. And we only held title to the office because of the great number of sheriff sales that helped the creditor class wipe the victims off the map. It is hard to say it, but we rejoiced when a sheriff sale was handed in. The fees were outrageously high—made so by the influence of the weekly papers on their legislators—but they were not too high for us. We did not think of the misery and despair it caused the victim of the commercial pirates—we only saw that it saved us from bankruptcy.

"After eighteen months of this struggle, Thompson concluded that it was not as good as wages. We had 78 cents a day each to live on, after keeping up the office, and had not paid the original note signed by the county officers. So I traded him an old silver watch and gave him my note for $25 and took his share of the plant.

"Then commenced the most terrific struggle of my existence. To my poverty was added the anxiety and fear of being unable to meet my obligations. I worked from eighteen to twenty hours a day.

"My relief came from the most unexpected source. One day a proposition from the White Sewing Machine Co., of Cleveland, Ohio, floated into the office offering a $65 machine for a quarter column advertisement and $16.25 cash. The advertisement was easy, but the cash was something out of my reach. Besides, the machine was a new one and just on the market, having bobbed up on the expiration of the patents that the Singer Company had controlled and which patents had kept all others from making machines. I knew that the wife of the village blacksmith, Chas. Rochat, wanted a machine, and I took the proposition to him and told him if he would risk it and send the money I would sell him the machine for $35, and that if the machine was not satisfactory I would not ask him anything, and he would get whatever machine it was for the $17 including the freight. He took the proposition. The machine came on time and was a beauty, and worked like a charm. They were delighted with it and paid me the balance, which was for the advertisement. This was so easy that I wrote the White people that I would like to have another machine on the same terms, but they said they didn't care to run another ad., while that was paid for, but that they would sell me the machines without any advertising for $16.50 each!

I saw that they had counted the advertisement at only 25 cents! I was surprised at the cheapness of the machine, as machines had been sold for $65 to $100 that were not better, and none could be had for less. To make a long story short, I bought and sold machines, making $15 to $20 on each, and then selling them for half what the people had been paying for them. I was soon out of debt and improved my office, and as the effect of the panic was gradually lessened, I soon found my office paying well. My intense struggle for bread was over.

"Having accumulated something over a thousand dollars in cash besides having a very well fitted up country office, I married in 1877 and concluded to go west and grow up with the country. My first wife's maiden name was Etta Bevan. My office, I leased to O. F. Thum, whom I had almost raised, and my wife having an aunt in Harrisonville, Mo., I located there in November, 1877. I bought an interest in the leading Democratic paper of the county, the *Register,* of its owner, Jas. H. Payne, but as soon as the other Democratic editors found I was a Republican, they made it hot for the county officials who gave us any patronage. Payne was one of the whitest men I ever had dealings with. He was an ex-Confederate soldier, and this opened my eyes to the fact that the rebels were not all bad people as I had always thought. When the Republicans of the county learned that I was a Republican they urged me to establish a Republican paper, and raised the money and gave it to me to go to St. Louis and buy the material. I sold my interest to Payne and began the publication of the *Cass News,* which is still running. There were about 1,700 Republican voters in the county and they supported that paper with a vengeance. I made it rather warm for the Democrats, and the ring of grafters that controlled the party and everybody wanted to read the sheet. It soon had a larger circulation than any other paper in the county, and it was a better paying property than even the two official papers. I was appointed postmaster under Hayes' administration, but resigned the office after several months, sold the *News* and went back to Indiana, and bought my old office back, having sold it in the meantime. This was in 1881. While I was in Harrisonville I cleared up several thousand dollars. I had more experience, and laid out plans to surprise the Hoosiers by putting in a modern country office, including a cylinder and job press, which the county never had.

"The old paper was a stock company and was poor property, but I bought up the stock to get it out of the way. I made a good stroke in this move, and cleared up several thousand dollars in thirteen months, by applying the experience I had gained in Missouri. But the old home wasn't the same to me as before I left it, and so I sold the paper out for much less than its real worth and in the spring of 1882 moved to Pueblo, Colo.

"Here I started a weekly local paper, with Lon Hoding of Madison, Ind., and an old schoolmate, J. H. Tyson. This brought me into an entirely new field and I wiggled along with it, carrying the whole financial load, until the other two concluded there was not a living in it for us all, and quit. They had no investment. I kept the paper going for about two years and concluded that I had to drop it, or all I had, so I traded it for a job printing outfit, donned an apron and went to work with a desperation born of necessity. I had some income from property in Missouri, and this saved me. I soon got the swing of the job printing business and it grew faster than I could get the facilities for handling it. I was soon out of debt again, bought more material, moved into larger quarters and found my bank account increasing to very satisfactory dimensions. My business was paying me about $100 a week net profits, and I felt that I would like to get away from the rent problem and get a better location than the one I was in, where I was cramped for room. With this idea I went on the main street and bought a building that could easily accommodate my plant. The place was leased and I could not get possession at once. Before I could get possession I sold the building, making about $2,000 clear on it. Then I bought another place and before I got a deed to it, property was advancing so rapidly on account of some new railroads and smelters, that I sold it and made $3,500, with only $100 paid down. The deed was finally made out direct to the party I sold to, so my name never entered into the matter. This deal kind of upset me, and made me feel that a business that was paying only $100 a week was poor stuff. I organized a company to handle my printing business and sold one-third the stock. I had observed enough not to allow a majority of stock to be in other hands. The office, under the new management which I turned over, never paid any dividends, but that was nothing to me for I had found a better way of making money through real estate and I made it in big chunks. I finally sold my interests in the stock to H. W. Young of Independence, Kansas. He was pretty hard to land, but I told him I would pay him $40 a week and turn the management over to him until he had satisfied himself that it was all I represented it to be. He was soon convinced and took it, and the business grew under his management very fast and became very profitable.

"About this time, 1890, I incidentally fell into a conversation about some strikes on the railroads, with Wm. Bradfield, an English shoemaker, who had a little shop on Union Avenue, and he gave me a pamphlet to read on the subject from the economic or Socialist viewpoint. He said it was the only copy he had and that he desired me to return it when read. I put it in my pocket and never thought about it until about a week or so later when I was trying to clean my pockets of the usual accumulation of notes and data that a real estate man gets, when I noted this leaflet. I read it and found it threw some new light upon the subject. I took it back to him and he questioned me to see whether I had really read it or not; finding I had, he suavely got me to take another economic tract. Thus he led me on, carefully avoiding any anxiety or pushing, for fear he would frighten me before I got the correct idea of what he was doing to me.

"To be brief, he 'landed' me good and hard. I saw a new light and found what I never knew existed. I saw what the increasing dullness meant and went into the financial study so thoroughly, that the result was, I closed up my real estate business and devoted my whole energies to the work of trying to get my neighbors to see the truths I had learned.

"I soon became convinced that another crisis was about to hit the country—

that the great capitalists wanted it and that they would benefit by it. I was scared. I owed several thousand dollars, though I had some very fine property. I began a desperate effort to turn my property into cash before the blow was struck. I sold at less than the market and soon got the reputation that I had lost my reason. This helped me to sell, for it convinced them that they were certainly getting bargains from a crazy man.

"When I tried to show Mr. Young and his partner that they were living over a volcano of depression they laughed at me. But they failed and lost their all. I had several very dear friends whom I tried to get to sell, but they only made sport of me.

"I was accumulating gold and greenbacks as rapidly as I sold property, and putting them into safety boxes which I had rented. One day I had a check for several thousand on the Western National Bank, Pueblo, and as usual demanded the money in gold. I told them they were gold standard men and should be given a taste of their own medicine. Mr. W. L. Graham, the president, as nice a man as one could meet, clean and honest, came around to the cashier's booth and said he would like to see me when I got through. So we went into his private office and he asked me what was the matter with me and the banks, referring to my denunciation of the banking system on the street corners. I told him the system was rotten, that it was an injury to the great mass of people, that it gave a few advantage over the many —which he denied but refused to enter into a discussion of the matter. He said I had come to that town without any capital, but I corrected him by saying that I had over $5,000 in cash and property. Well, he said I had come to the bank and had never been refused, even when my overchecks were considerable sums, to which I agreed, but pointed out to him that I was not under obligation to the bank, as they certainly had considered me good, and I had always paid them 12 per cent interest on every dollar of loan or overcheck. Not finding me vulnerable on this subject he said that every business man sometime had the need of more money than he could keep on hand, and asked me if I thought I was entitled to any favors from the banks, talking as I did against them. I told him I did not, that I had counted the cost of the step I had taken; that I had more real money at that moment than he had in his bank and that I would have money when his bank closed its doors. And I did, for his bank with others closed in the exciting days of the panic of 1893—some six months later.

"I now put my whole time in study and agitation. I got next to all the radicals, inspired them with new hope, printed and distributed leaflets by the tens of thousands on the streets and made myself a nuisance generally to my former business acquaintances. I told the owners of a labor paper, Flory and Donahue, that if they would let me control the reading matter I would edit their paper during the campaign for nothing and I made it as hot as I knew how, and increased its circulation from a few hundred non-paying subscribers to 2,700 paid ones in nine months. During the campaign of 1892 I paid $10 a day for two columns in an evening paper for the month before the election and it proved very effective for our ticket, the Populist, came in second. In fact, they offered me $5 a day to continue the work after the election, so good an effect it had on their circulation.

"But I had been considering the publication of a paper of my own, the idea originating in these two successes under my pen, and in February, 1893, I moved to Greensburg, Ind., to make the effort, because that was about the center of population and was near the great industrial centers of Chicago, St. Louis, Cincinnati, Cleveland and other places where I expected I would get the circulation. My ideal then was a circulation of 10,000 a week. That sounded very large to me. I knew I had enough money to run it several years even if it did not pay.

"But almost from the first my greatest circulation went to California and remained there until the last few years.

"The people of Greensburg ostracised me and my family, and made it very disagreeable, and that was one of the determining factors in my starting the colony at Tennessee City.

"I moved from Greensburg to Tennessee in July, 1894."

When Wayland left Pueblo, Colo., for Greensburg, Ind., to start the *Coming Nation*, he had approximately $80,-000 in gold and government bonds. The country was in a state of panic and banks were breaking on all sides, so, distrusting banking institutions, he buried his treasure in a woodshed at his home.

He had now made sufficient money, the income of which would support his family. He was thoroughly converted to socialism and resolved to give his energies to publishing a paper in which to express his ideas. He had no thought of making money with this newspaper but merely wanted it to pay its way. This has been his thought during the 18 years that he has been publishing a socialist newspaper.

The *Coming Nation* astonished him in its growth. At this time the Populist party was in its zenith. There was coming a line of cleavage in the party. The leaders were becoming conservative and the rank and file radical. The Populist newspapers were following the lead of the party public officials, and becoming less radical in thought. The new paper fitted into the times. While the *Coming Nation* was never a Populist paper it appealed to the Populists, especially the radical brand.

At this time two books were written and widely circulated which had a great influence on the public mind. One of these was Bellamy's Looking Backward, an optimistic picture of the future co-operative society. The other was Donnelly's Caesar's Column, a picture of commercial society fully developed and it was as pessimistic as the other book was optimistic. Most active Populists had read these books. The *Coming Nation*, therefore, needed but to be introduced to the Populists in order to get subscriptions. It is not surprising in view of the state of the public mind that the paper quickly attained a circulation of 65,000 and that largely among the Populists.

Not long after Wayland started the *Coming Nation* he conceived the idea of organizing a co-operative colony. It was characteristic of the man and his vision. At this time Wayland had not read the classic works of Marks and Engels and his socialist philosophy was decidedly Utopian. Had he begun as we begin today, he would not have made the colony mistake. Still we doubt if he ever would have done the work he has done without having first caught the vision of the Utopian side of socialism, because the Utopian has been the untiring propagandist of the movement. Ruskin colony was organized in 1894, near Tennessee City, Tenn., and the *Coming Nation* moved to the colony quarters where it was published as a part of the business of the colony.

Wayland discovered his mistake almost immediately on going to the colony, but he turned over the ownership of the paper that he had built up and when he found himself unable to agree with the colonists he left them on the 22nd day of July, 1895, much poorer in cash, but wiser in experience.

He went to Kansas City, Mo., where on the 31st day of August, 1895, the first issue of the *Appeal* appeared. So many people invaded his office at Kansas City simply to converse with him that he decided to withdraw from a big city and go to a small town; accordingly on the 6th day of February, 1897, the *Appeal* began to issue in Girard, Kansas, its present home.

The birth of the *Appeal* was not under such auspicious conditions as that of the *Coming Nation*. The silver craze had taken hold of the People's Party and that party was turning to fusion. Wayland took with him from Tennessee no mailing list and the *Appeal* had to start at the bottom, just as the *Coming Nation* had done two years before.

When the Populist party fused with the Democrats, Wayland cut entirely adrift from it and made a straight declaration for socialism. The country was crazy over the silver question and subscribers for a socialist paper were hard to get. The circulation in 1896 fell off rapidly, but began to grow again after the campaign, when the betrayed and disappointed Populists began to gather to its support. Populism had been given its death blow by fusion just as Wayland had predicted, and the most radical of the Populists began to espouse socialism. The circulation of the paper increased slowly until the war with Spain, when the country once more went wild and the circulation of the *Appeal* sagged again, and the receipts of the paper did not equal the expenses. During these early years of the *Appeal*, salaries as you may imagine were very low to all concerned with the paper and before the *Appeal* became a self-supporting institution, a large chunk of the original $80,000 that Wayland took to Greensburg had been used up.

The history of the *Appeal* is sufficiently familiar to the readers of this book and nothing on this subject need be said.

Wayland's home life has been saddened by the death of both his first and second wives. The first wife, mother of his five living children, died on October 5th, 1898. He was married again to a Girard lady, Pearl Hunt, April 10th, 1901, who on the 9th day of June, 1911, was killed in an automobile accident. Of the five children, John Wayland is at this writing studying law in Emporia, Walter is cashier in the *Appeal* office, Ollie, the oldest, is her father's housekeeper, and the two youngest, Julia and Edith, are in college.

Wayland's prescience is great and his predictions of the future have been very accurate. In this connection, we publish below several editorials and miscellaneous articles, all of which will be interesting to those who have passed through the stirring days of socialist history with Wayland and the *Appeal*.

LEAVES OF LIFE.

By J. A. Wayland

Criticisms and inquiries why I use the soubriquet "One Hoss" have been coming in much of late. While in Pueblo, Colo., I operated a small job printing office. I had only a few fonts of type and one little press and my competitors were well supplied with all modern conveniences. I had to make a living and I went to work to get it. I named the office the "one-hoss print shop" and used it as an imprint. I used the above wood cut on my envelopes and letter heads. I never abandoned the plebeian appellation, although in four years the business grew to occupy a brick block of its own full of presses of best make. I am not ashamed of the record. I worked physically and mentally and am proud of it. After that I made thousands of dollars speculating in real estate but that is nothing to be proud of. My critics fear the vulgarism of "one hoss" will detract. I write to the laboring classes who are not shocked at such expressions. I am one of them and proud of that. Dull as they are they are the salt of the earth and any reform that ever comes must come through them. To them I have given all that I have, all that I am and all that I may be, and by them I expect to be misunderstood. But in my own way I shall lecture them and explain to them and exhort them to better conditions. I would not give much for the culture, refinement and thoughtfulness of those who fail to understand the one-hoss.

ON DEBS' RELEASE FROM WOODSTOCK JAIL IN 1895.

Few men have received an ovation equal to that given E. V. Debs at Chicago last week—not to Debs the individual, but to Debs the embodiment of resistance to tyranny, resistance to usurpation, to Debs the patriot. It was not the homage of slaves to power and glitter, not the bending of the servile knee to master, not the fawning to be followed by favors, but the spontaneous outflow of honor from sincere hearts for one who prefers fetters to gilded freedom, liberty to life. Debs is a type of manhood to be honored. In all ages of the world such men have been crucified, burned, hanged, and murdered by the ruling powers of despotism such as now control this nation through the power of wealth over ignorant and superstitious masses. Debs, is a name that will be written high among the greatest names of the earth, to designate great spirits who lived and loved liberty above power, knowledge above riches, justice above property. In the struggle ahead of the working people to throw off the galling bonds of industrial and wage-slavery, when the future historian chronicles this period, the name of Debs will be a great central figure. He is the wisest student of men and nature, who has attempted to lead the working people in modern times. That the ruling powers malign and ridicule him is the best possible evidence of his true merit, and that what he advocates is not a theory that can be used by the idlers of the world for their benefit. All hail to Debs.

WHAT DEBS THOUGHT OF THE APPEAL IN 1899.

DEAR COMRADE:—I heartily congratulate you upon the great work of the *Appeal* in every part of the country. During the past few months I have been in most of the states of the Union and in every village, town and city I have been welcomed by the *Appeal*. Its friendly face appears everywhere. It is literally honey-combing capitalism. Wherever the *Appeal* is at work, and that seems everywhere, socialism has at least a nucleus and the light is spreading. You have a faculty of reaching the average man. More than anything else it is your pointed paragraphs that do the work. More power to the *Appeal*.

EUGENE V. DEBS.

Xenia, O., June 6, 1899.

OPINION OF GOMPERS IN 1896.

A correspondent takes me to task for a criticism of Mr. Gompers. I had like strictures or criticism of Mr. Powderly, too, years ago but I knew then as now he was a traitor to the laboring people. The very clipping my friend sends me, quoting Mr. Gompers, contains the proof of his infidelity to labor. It shows he knows the socialist theory, uses the part that tickles labor, but only to lure labor into the hands of its enemies. A man is a fool or a knave who tells labor it creates all wealth and then refuses to advise or show labor that only by capturing the government and the putting of wealth into the possession of all the people collectively can the injustice be remedied. Mr. Gompers, in my humble opinion, is one of the ablest generals that capitalists have. Of course, he must make a pretense of fighting capitalists else he could not hold his job. The man who can mislead labor can always be a financial success. Mr. Arthur of the Locomotive Engineer Brotherhood is another shining example like Powderly and Gompers.

THE CHICAGO CONVENTION IN 1896.

Well, the Chicago convention has met and done its work. The cunning hands of the goldbugs, while they could not stem the revolt or name the candidates, have had much to do with the platform. True, it declares for silver and against bank paper, but it demands that all paper money must be redeemed in coin. It is not a step in advance of the platforms of the last century. In effect, it says, the United States can not make money, except it prints it on gold or silver, and he or they who can control its gold and silver can thus control the volume of money and expand or contract it at their pleasure. It has no demand for the public ownership of railroads that are fast sweeping the little remaining property from the people into the possession of the millionaires. It has no word for the public ownership of the telegraph by which alone a free and independent press is possible. It has no word for postal savings banks to furnish a safe place for the people to deposit their money where it will not be lost by dishonest or venturesome bankers. It has no word for doing justice to the millions lies, except to grant greater powers to an interstate commission which is and will be appointed by the trusts. It has no word for doing justice to the millions of homeless Americans who have no right to live a day in the United States except they buy the privilege from some landlord. It has a lot of flap-doodle that doesn't do any harm to the vested interests of capital. On this document, created to catch the men who believe free silver coinage is the panacea of all ills, they have nominated Mr. Bryan, of Nebraska, a man much better than the platform, and one they expect to disorganize the Peoples' party by a general stampede.

If this occurs the Peoples' Party is a thing of the past. In four years the two old parties will have the field to themselves and will do as they please and if the reformers find themselves left with organization to assist, they can lay the blame where it belongs—fusion and death. The Greenback party was killed and got out of the way. When out of the way the old parties pursued their old methods. They will do it again.

THE APPEAL AND THE CAMPAIGN OF 1896.

The *Appeal* has been and is a financial failure, but it is proving a success as an educator. After the campaign is over and the property class has again gathered the harvest of deluded voters on the money question as they have for thirty years on the tariff and other by-plays, the *Appeal* will be sought by those who have discovered how they have been taken in, and will go ahead. I realize as well as any one that the people are going to discuss the finance question—a phase of it only—and will again be delivered unto plutocracy. But some progress in economic knowledge among the masses will be made that will be an advance. The people are woefully ignorant of what power, the character and control of money, is. This will lead millions to further investigation and unfold the great truths that lie just below the surface. To me this is like going to England to get to San Francisco, but if people believe that is the only route it is better than not going at all, for I know, as does every student of sociology, that *there is no money question in a rightly organized society.* It is a waste of time and energy if the main question could be gotten at directly.

So in the present campaign the *Appeal* will keep right in the track it has been following, turning neither to the right or left, smiling on the execrations of the dupes of the old parties and the money reformers alike—for they both give me the deuce. I see little hope of any good coming to a nation before a large bad spell shall have gone through. I see a struggle coming, no matter which side wins in this fight. And when that awful time breaks on the nation the position of the *Appeal* will be appreciated —for the banners of manhood vs. property rights will prove that its position has been right. The money question is just the skirmish of the real battle that is to follow. All these surface questions are but the bubbles that rise up from the bottom—the cause is monopoly or private ownership. That is the real question in this campaign, but only a few realize it.

"You can't eat your cake and have it," is a favorite maxim with the idle class when they illustrate the poverty of their fellow man by saying he spends it for whisky and useless objects. Granted. But does not the usurer eat up his loan by the interest he receives and then have the original cake of capital returned to him intact? The laboring man who spends his wages foolishly, spends his own wages, not that robbed from the toil of his brother.

THE way to succeed is never to let up.

IF it were not for the poor people how would the rich people get along? Riches would bring no servants unless a system can obtain that will keep a portion of the people on the borders of want. The poor people are kept so, that the monopolists may have menials to do their bidding. The poor could get along without the idle rich, but how would the rich get along?

MONKEY'S DON'T.

Man raises meats for idlers. Monkeys don't.

Man builds mansions for idlers. Monkeys don't.

Man creates money for use of idlers. Monkeys don't.

Man labors that others may idle. Monkeys don't.

Man starves that idlers may surfeit. Monkeys don't.

Man freezes that idlers may be warm. Monkeys don't.

Man plows and produces for idlers. Monkeys don't.

Man tends flocks for wool for idlers. Monkeys don't.

Man makes bad laws, laws that keep him in servitude. Monkeys don't.

If the men who plow, tend flocks, herd cattle, build mansions, starve, freeze and make laws were only as wise as monkeys what a glorious world this would be!

There are never two sides to RIGHT.

The usurer is the only one who can eat his pie and still have it.

The public, north and south, hung John Brown, not in effigy, but in person. He was a crank and a dangerous man. But the very criminals who permitted his execution, criminals, I say, because such are the men who would suppress free speech and thus compel men who differ with them in ideas to appeal to force—these men have taught their children to sing peans of praise to the memory of John Brown, "whose soul goes marching on." One generation murders people who hold ideas in advance of them, and the next generation makes deities of them. What fools these mortals be. Few men who read this will think they are referred to, but that some one else is the fool, but all of us are more or less afflicted with this blighting malady.

If all the wealth of the nation were the property of a dozen men, all the rest propertyless, would the nation be rich? If all were supplied with an abundance the nation would undoubtedly be rich. In proportion as the many are poor and the few rich the nation is poor. The richest have never earned an honest crust of bread. They have robbed the balance by process of law.

Great fortunes are the fathers of anarchy.

Epicurus, who lived before Christ, said to a friend, "You ask what advance I have made? I am beginning to be a friend to myself." This was the result of his study. He considered it an evidence of dawning knowledge. Reader, do you think those who will kill and rob for a king are friends to themselves? Do they know the wrongs they do? Are you, living under the light of this century, who vote to perpetuate a system that protects trusts, monopolies and other legalized robberies, friends to yourselves? Will you not profit by the accumulated knowledge of ages? Are not the results of our legalized robberies of today just the same as those brutal soldiers of a brutal king—the oppression and robbery of the people? If this republic is to be saved, the people must begin to be friends to themselves.

It will avail the laborers naught to elect one of their number to office if he does not understand the social question. An ignorant laborer can do no good in office. He is as soft a snap as capitalists want. Elect working men, but elect socialists.

Greed will exist as long as it can find food. Therefore cut off the food supply by making all the means of production public property without profits and greed will die and love will take its place.

The wisest men that ever lived spent

their lives in studying what is now termed political economy. It was that study that made them wise. The truths they discovered are as if they never had been discovered to the masses of mankind. It has ever been to the interest of the rulers and the rich to keep the masses in ignorance of the demonstrations of philosophers and thinkers.

THE longer you submit to unjust conditions the harder it will be to change them.

WHEN any great calamity befalls any portion of our country that the people are starving and freezing or prostrated with disease, neither state nor national government can do anything, but proclamations for charity are issued. But when capital has its privileges challenged—then sound the bugle, put all the machinery in force, call for the sheriff and posse, speed the thumb-hanging militia and its gatling guns, march forth the national army, call the legislature and congress, vote money and treasure, and bond the people into deeper bondage. O this government of the people by the rich, for the rich, is a dandy. The poor suckers ain't in it.

The wisest men I have ever met have been poor. This is self-evident, for if they had given their every thought to money making, they would have had no time or inclination to study the thoughts of philosophers.

Debt is like morphine. You borrow and things go smoothly, but to repay leaves the victim in added distress, and the amount with interest is renewed. Few men who once indulge in debt and interest are ever free, but go through life a slave to money loaners. It is as hard to break as the morphine habit, and the millions of wrecked lives attest the poison of the interest taker. It is a crime against God and man. A people in debt is helpless. The usurers make the laws and keep them in bondage. Freedom is impossible so long as there is debt.

None of us possess all of wisdom, nor can possess all, but the trouble lies in the fact that so few care to possess any.

There is no escaping this one fact that a bond means somebody is in bondage. A bond on land would be worth nothing if no one would use the land. People would kick if the bond were written against their persons, but by telling them it is on land or the nation or the state or the city, they will pay the interest right along. O! the people are so wise!

You are not going to get something for nothing and get it honestly. Neither are you going to get something for work that in itself produces nothing and get that something honestly. You must *produce* something yourself, or aid in its production at some stage to be entitled to something honestly. The teacher who produces useful knowledge in a child or a man is a producer, but if it is base ideas he teaches he is not a producer but a destroyer and is entitled to no reward, but punishment. Work does not entitle a man to reward unless it is good work. All useless or ill-directed labor is criminal.

There is a little article that everybody uses, and yet I never see it advertised. I look over the daily and weekly press in vain to find where it can be purchased. On this they are as silent as the tomb. In vain I look at the signs on the street, or in the shop windows for it. It is sold in every village and hamlet in the land, and yet no drummer ever carries samples of it and never takes an order for it. Its price never raises, and yet it pays handsomely all who deal in it. And strange to say there is usually but one place in a town that keeps it. There is always a supply of it—never too much nor too little. It is never taxed, no matter how many thousands dollars' worth are in stock. There has never been any corner or speculation in it and its price at wholesale or retail is always just the same. It has never made a millionaire or a pauper. That little thing is a postage stamp, and if all articles were produced and handled in the same way, there would be neither poverty, crime nor insanity in the United States. Try it.

ONE working man is worth a world full of men who live off rent, profit or interest.

LAND, houses, machinery and money will not sustain life, but they are necessities that all men must have to create what does sustain life. So if people permit these things to be owned by individuals, the cunning or dishonest, a few will eventually get control of them and live in luxury off the labor of those who do use them in producing wealth. The only safe, the only sensible plan, is to have this common property, accessible to all on exactly the same conditions, and then a few cannot use them to profit off the many. Any other policy is suicidal, as the present conditions show.

WHEN we violate the laws of nature pain results. When the laws of truth and harmony are violated the pains that follow are warnings that must be heeded, and they will remain until the causes are removed or modified. The present social agony is the debt people have to pay for social injustice done in the past. It has been produced by political ignorance and can be removed by political wisdom, which must come from the people themselves.

A DOLLAR a day is enough for a working man, but a hundred thousand a day is not enough for monopolists or landlords. This is the system that working men vote for, and then wander submissively over the land trying to sell themselves to some of these rich employers. Socialism would change all this, and the monopolist would not be in it.

This government is just as wise and good as the majority of the people—no better, no worse. Ignorant people elect ignorant or corrupt officials who make ignorant or venal laws. It will never be better until the people are taught better.

It takes several days to tame an elephant and make it submissive to any conditions that may be imposed upon it. When men are to be enslaved, the cunning proceed by an even slower process, using years teaching children, and finally all the people are submissively groveling in poverty that the few may surfeit in unearned luxury.

Some people tell me I am a dreamer, an optimist. Others tell me I am a pessimist. Both oppose my ideas and neither of them know what I am. Both are positive they are right, but both cannot be right, for their views are opposite. It never occurs to either of them that one of them must be and both of them *may* be wrong. Funny people in this revolving old world.

It is not the men who have a good home and work at fair wages that commit the crimes of the day, but men who have no home and no work, or men who have other men's homes and do no useful work. This being true, and none can successfully deny it, is it not the part of wisdom to so arrange the social fabric that all men may have work and that none may own the home of another? Is it the part of wisdom to have conditions that produce crime? Do you expect peace when you make peace impossible? Every poorhouse cries out against your system, every jail cries out against your system, every penitentiary cries out against your system, every ragged or hungry child cries out against your system, every drunkard cries out against your system, and the idle rich or the mischievously busy rich, who have been the cause of all these woes, are a standing indictment of this social anarchy.

TICK, tick, tick. The clock on the mantel above me never ceases to remind me that time ceases not, no matter if to humanity affairs go ill or well. And they go ill fast enough. Who would have predicted twenty-five years ago that the nation would be flooded with poverty-stricken people facing a condition far more serious than that which it had just passed through? A few men cried aloud yes, but words of warning were unheeded, they were jeered at and derided, were crushed out of business and the mad, thoughtless multitude rushed pell-mell in its wild struggle to make money. A few have the money and wealth, the many have poverty and woe. All this is the result of vicious legislation, and the debt of ignorance and greed will not be paid until the nation returns to ways of justice through sackcloth and ashes. The sun shines, the showers fall, man's mechanical ingenuity is fruitful, but the millions are in want and woe because they refuse to seek the ways of justice and recognize the rights of their brothers. Every man for himself is the method, starvation and crime the result. In a few more years there will be more results. The world and all in it changes constantly, and the future looks ominous. And the clock says tick, tick, tick. Can you interpret it?

A POLITICALLY prejudiced man is like a dull school boy—so hard to get a correct principle in his head.

When a tenant gives his landlord half, and out of the balance pays his taxes, the merchant's and the monopolist's profit, you wonder why he is poor? I don't.

Two classes are satisfied with conditions—those who have been brutalized by work and poverty and those who live pretty well off other people's toil. To which do you belong?

A small landlord or a small money lender is just as exacting as greater ones. Do away with a system that makes it a necessity for one set of humans to buy the use of land or money from another set.

How often have the philosophers of the world given you good advice and you refused to listen but when chasing after the politicians? Well, you are down in the ditch, covered with just the mire you made, and there you will remain until you learn some truth.

How can a man who produces no wealth honestly have anything to exchange with a producer of wealth? Why do wealth producers have to keep up a class of men who produce nothing?

Why do producers of wealth have to go to non-producers for the privilege of working? Why do producers have little wealth and non-producers much wealth? Why cannot producers exchange wealth with each other to supply their wants? And why do they have to go to non-producers for that privilege? Why are producers unable to put their price on their labor or products? And how comes it that non-producers have the power to arrange those prices? If you can answer these satisfactorily, so as to uphold the present social system, you are a dandy.

CRIME increases as poverty increases. Poverty increases as more profits are taken from the workers, whether by interest, taxes or rent. If the nation operated the industries neither interest, rent nor profit would exist. The nation, state and city will operate industries and employ all people when the workers vote for it. The workers will vote for it when they understand the principle and they will understand the principle when socialists teach them.

EVERY step of progress in the world's history has been made in peace.

Thoughts that elevate mankind are not generated by strife.

LABOR has learned to make everything necessary to happify the human family—except laws. The schemers make the laws and by them rob the workers into poverty.

The postoffice is socialistic.
The public schools system is socialistic.
The public roads are socialistic.
The public streets are socialistic.
The public sewers are socialistic.
The court house is socialistic.
The State house is socialistic.
The libraries are socialistic.
The express company is not socialistic.
The railroads are not socialistic.
The toll pike is not socialistic.
The coal business is not socialistic.
The oil business is not socialistic.
The meat business is not socialistic.
The sugar business is not socialistic.
The banking business is not socialistic.

How does a king secure obedience? Why do the people pay taxes to support him in dazzling extravagance and go in want themselves? Did you ever think of it? Is it not ridiculous, absurd, disgusting, that some drunken debauche is looked upon as a little god? Alone he couldn't do it a minute. But he has given power and place to some men and called them barons, others dukes, others lords, others this, that and the other. Each of these in turn have special privileges and an influence and the same theory, lessening in degree, goes down to the foreman of a factory or the boss of the stable. These have the influence to keep the many in line to support their kind, for if the king falls they all tumble. All kings or rulers have an offensive and defensive alliance with the churches. Churches in every land support royalty for a price. Without the aid of the church kingdoms would tumble. What of it? Just change the king idea for the president and see how it looks.

THE income of European lords and barons comes from ground rent. Does not the income of our lords come from the same source? What is the difference? Can't you see that in each case the many work and the few enjoy it?

It is not the mere title of lord that brings an income. He must be lord of something that people must have, and pay him for. Thus in Europe he is lord of the land; here he is the landlord, or trust lord. If these people oppress the workers in Europe, do they not do the same in this country? Can't you see that you are oppressed by the laws that protect a few in the possession of the soil they do not till? Or the railroad you, not they, operate? There is no phase of oppression in Europe that is not present in America. Think over it and see if you can conjure up any different condition.

I LIKE private enterprises and private property! They are so adequate in an emergency. Now out in Western Nebraska is a good illustration. They have private property, of course, and are starving and freezing to death. Then private enterprise steps in, organizes charities and tries to raise funds to feed them! It is so nice when you are dying of starvation and cold to wait several weeks while people are harangued by organized charity beggars to get you something to eat! It is better to starve and freeze and hold on to private property and private enterprise instead of having the government organized to employ people and see that they have an abundance if they will do their share of work. Those who don't do any work, who get all the wealth, advise the people against using the government to help themselves. These rich now have all the use of the government. The government gives them fat contracts and pours millions into the hands of a few, but it would be rank paternalism—treason—to suggest that the nation should send food and coal to the sufferers in Western Nebraska! You see it would interfere with the rich showing their generosity and developing their benevolence! In one end of a state wheat being fed to hogs and in the other human beings starving! O! most glorious civilization! Adorable system of intelligence and progress!! Supremest of all earthly ideas of order and harmony! Fat pigs and starving babies!! Millions for balls and banquets and military—emaciated and dead bodies of citizens starved on western prairies where they were trying to make an honest living! Praise your government, O, ye workers.

"IF the laboring people are satisfied, why not let them alone? Why try to create dissatisfaction?" I will answer it by asking: The chattel slaves were ignorant and satisfied, why agitate and have a bloody war to change their conditions? The ruling classes were satisfied under King George; therefore it was wrong for Patrick Henry, Thomas Paine, Thomas Jefferson and a few other agitators to make them dissatisfied. If a thing is wrong it must perish and the fruit of the upas tree called "civilization" shows it to be fundamentally wrong and it must perish. Newer, higher ideas and aspirations are taking hold of the people and there will be no peace until these ideas are a part of the social system—until wage slavery is wiped off the face of the earth.

IF a man were to get a boy to put his tongue on a piece of frosty iron on a cold morning to see how hot it is, and the boy thereby lost a coating of his tongue by the contact, as I did, do you think he could fool that boy again in that way? Not much. But you voters lose some of your reason as you grow older, and for thirty years the old party politicians have been fooling you at every election and you always come up smiling and credulous at the next election to get the skin taken off you. You don't, eh? Yes, but you do. Not only the skin, but the food, clothing and homes have been taken from you by the repetition, and there are millions of you so hungry and discouraged you don't know where you are going to sleep at night, or words to that effect. Why don't you reason as much as a boy? You never got any benefit of a vote in your miserable existence, yet you will persist in sticking your ballot on that same political iron to get burned. You are a sunflower, and no mistake.

WHAT a picnic life is to us farmers, mechanics and laboring people generally! One continual round of pleasure from the cradle to the grave! Our work of a few hours daily is sweetened by the anticipation of the pleasures to follow, and really is no work at all. We know when our time is done we can go to our beautiful home, and be met at the door by our wives and children, and have a magnificent banquet under the glare of the electric chandeliers. And after tea we can don our clawhammer coats and immaculate shirt front with diamonds and either go to the opera, party or entertain our friends in our magnificent parlors. Silks and diamonds flash, wine glasses tinkle, and the hours are whiled away like a fairy dream while our coachmen on the outside await orders of the assembled guests. What have we to complain of? No wonder we working people are so well satisfied and frown down on anyone who suggests that the good old Democratic and Republican parties should be discarded—those parties that have made life so pleasant for us. What a lovely picnic life is to us working people!

Do you wonder at men failing and losing their property? Why should you? How do you suppose millionaires get the property they possess if somebody does not lose it? Do you suppose that their wealth comes to them out of the clouds; that other men do not lose what they gain? Can a king have power without curtailing the liberty of the people? No; nor can a monopoly gain wealth unless other people create and lose it.

IN feudal days the poor had to work for the rich and powerful or be killed. Today they, the poor, have to work for the rich or be starved.

Where is the ultimate difference?

In the feudal days the poor supported the rich in power by physical force. Today the poor support the rich in power by ballots.

Where is the ultimate difference?

In the feudal days the poor lived in hovels and rags that the rulers might live in palaces and purple. Today the poor do the same thing.

Where is the difference?

In the feudal days the poor were the servants and menials of the rich. Today the poor are the same servants and menials.

Where is the difference?

In the feudal days the poor could have deposed their oppressors if they had not been so ignorant, suspicious and disorganized. Today they could depose their oppressors but for the same reason.

Where is the difference?

In feudal days anybody willing to work could find a master. Today they cannot.

Here is the difference.

Don't you believe the masses in the feudal days, by their life and actions, were veritable fools?

You have so many theories, plans and propositions presented to you that you become bewildered and hopeless of what is best to do. There is, if you would stop to think, just one proper thing to do that cannot fail the best results and accomplishing that which is best. Study the best thinkers and teach your neighbors. In due course this will bear fruit in some definite line of action. No good thought absorbed is ever lost, no truth spoken that will not bear fruit according to its kind. Lay siege to your neighbors, each according to his disposition and prejudice. So long as you have neighbors who are deficient in knowledge you possess, you have work to do. This will in time have its influence on county, state and nation. Do not think the effort wasted because you fear you will not live to see results. Our lives are but atoms—remember millions are to follow us. What we now enjoy in freedom others gave their lives for. They did not shirk because they might not realize results. Look back over the dark ages when to think was a crime and to speak the truth about church and state meant death, when even the rulers could neither read nor write, much less the serfs and slaves, our ancestors. Think how precious one truth spoken must have been. Remember, George Washington was a strong adherent of King George and monarchy until he was converted. To the utmost of your power and purse spread the light of the New Civilization. Do not think time and money wasted on even the poor and unlettered. They are often as potent as men of means. Many untutored men have subdued nations. Never let a day go by without sowing the seed of discontent with the present unjust social conditions. Do your best. The future will take care of itself.

It matters not how sincere and honest any man is, if what he advocates is wrong its injury will be none the less. An honest man is not necessarily a wise man. An honest, sincere man may be a Christian, a Mohammedan, a Buddhist or an agnostic, but a wise man cannot be all of these. Then how are wise men to be distinguished? By throwing overboard prejudice and bigotry and listening to all with equal willingness to believe what proves itself to your reason as being best. "Error is harmless when truth is free to combat it," but if you get prejudiced to some theory or men and refuse to investigate, and weigh criticism on their merits, you can never see their errors. If they are right no sophistry or twisting can deceive you. If they are wrong, the injury they will do will be none the less because they are honest. Honest men are deceived by frauds, charlatans and schemers, but just as a man is deceived so is he not wise.

WHEN the king appoints the judges the judges decide for the king. When the rich make the president and the president appoints the judges, for whom will the judge decide?

WHAT pleasure a farmer must take

in toiling all day in the hot sun producing raw material which the capitalist class, through another band of serfs called wage-earners, work into the finished product, and then sell at an enormous profit. For every drop of sweat there is a cool shade, a dinner party, a monkey banquet, a junketing trip through Europe, a titled wedding, or some other demoralizing event for the idle posterity of the capitalist class.

How pleasant it is to be able to make someone do all the serving work of the world while you have nothing to do but hunt for amusement. How sad it is that the working class is so senseless as to stagger along under the load which capitalism has strapped on its back, when socialism would take the load off and make the capitalist help carry it.

THE people are trained like so many animals by their masters to spurn the idea of "dividing up" while at the same time their masters are dividing up all the people make among themselves. Of the wealth produced by the people each year the masters divide it among themselves and leave the people only about enough to keep them in working condition. They are practicing the "dividing up" principle on the people all the time, and the people are so stupid they don't see it. The socialist proposes to abolish such dividing up and making it impossible for the idlers to get any of the wealth the workers produce. It is amusing to hear a poor devil who has not a decent suit of clothes to his back who has been dividing up with capitalists all his life opposing socialism because he don't want to "divide up" when he has nothing to divide up but his rags. But there are lots of them.

If you are a loafer I am not talking to you. If you work with hands and brain, do you have all good things of life to which your labor in the social hive entitles you? That is the political question. It is a matter of politics whether you know it or not. Politics controls industry. By politics you can organize industry on a basis that will give each worker the full result of his or her labor. The capitalists control politics in order to prevent this being done. If those who are doing useful work received all the results of useful work their pay would be equal to more than $2,500 a year in wealth. And why should they not have it if they produce it? Why should schemers get anything? Do you believe that workers are not entitled to the best houses, best food and best clothing? If not, why not?

"MASTER AND MAN" has had many forms, but capitalism leaves Man the most helpless. In any other form of servitude the man could flee to some other country and escape, but capitalism has all countries and Man is denied food and shelter except he submits to the mastership of capital.

THE chattel slave made every effort to escape from the man who furnished him work, food, clothes and a shanty. The wage slave, on the contrary, stands in constant dread of having his master tell him to go. Wage slavery is the most effective system ever devised.

IF the capitalists of this or any other land made the earth I could see why they owned it. If they made the houses and machinery, I could see why they own them. If they made the food and clothing I could see why they own them.

But as God made the earth, and laboring people made the other things mentioned, I cannot see any equity in any other ownership than in them. It is really hard to believe that capitalists have persuaded all the producers of wealth that they, not the makers, should be entitled to them.

Do you want to be a nothing in life—a bubble—just like the millions of bubbles, a wage slave just like the billions of wage slaves that have existed in the centuries behind us? If not, get an idea different from the ideas that have and do control the masses and keep them as they are. If the idea you grasp is great and true, and you propagate it and agitate it, so will you be as a wave is to the bubble on its bosom. Any man can make the world better for his living if imbued with a true idea. One man can do much if he tries. Life is for something higher and nobler than a birth to death struggle after what is termed property.

THE rich man's horses are better housed and cared for than the working people from whose labor the rich man is fed, clothed and entertained. A comparison of the stables of the rich and the homes of the workers ought to make the voters ashamed to support a system by their votes that reduces them below the level of a horse. But a long period of education has made the people look upon this as a matter of course.

WHAT wonderful forethought on the part of the Supreme Being when He conceived the idea of leaving coal oil under the surface where the people couldn't find it until Rockefeller was born! The ways of the Infinite are inscrutable—as interpreted by the people today.

WHEN I see old soldiers and negroes doing service on the city rock pile, for being out of money, I wonder what the war was all about anyhow.

THE advocate for a criminal uses as much ingenuity in painting him white and the innocent black as he can, and so do the writers for the corporation and money kings.

A WASHINGTON woman has had a dentist put a gold filling in her dog's tooth "which glistens in the sunlight as perfectly as if it had been in the incisor of a human being." It would be awful to have human beings so situated that they could have their teeth filled when needed, but no matter, so the dogs of the rich can afford it. The woman's income is derived from profit based on private ownership and the poor also believe in that system.

Why do kings and emperors and nobles and monopolists and capitalists oppose socialism? Why, in the interest of the poor, dear working people, of course. Don't they say so? What better evidence than their words and tears do you need? They would cry their eyes out to see the poor workers oppressed and robbed and made slaves of. Johnny, get your eyes open.

I never see a lot of young folks idling their time in aimlessness on the streets or trying to get amusement out of baseball or other games, but I think of the energy and earnestness that the monopolists are exercising to weave around these thoughtless ones the chains of industrial slavery. When these thoughtless youths grow up they will find monopoly has pre-empted every field and the bright dreams of their youth will sink into a struggle to exist. It is too bad but it delights the industrial barons. It is easy to rob a people who are thoughtless.

WHAT is the difference to a man whether he is held up by a footpad and relieved of his cash, or is arrested for exercising his natural rights and taken before the officers and they take his cash under the cover of a fine? In either instance he loses his money and those who take it from him get the benefit. It's different, you know, which way you do your robbing.

WHEN a poor old man marries you seldom if ever hear of his children kicking up a disturbance, but when a rich old man marries again, there is the deuce to pay. You see it is always property that causes the trouble. If all property were held public the peace of families would be greatly increased. Under this system children can hardly wait for their parents to die so they will get possession of what they have neither earned nor gathered. Private riches have been a curse rather than a blessing to their possessors.

THERE is nothing more pitiful than a man who is satisfied to give his best abilities to enrich a corporation and then believe that corporations are to be commended for furnishing employment.

WHEN I read about the treatment of the unemployed, the convicts who are leased out for private profit and the misdoings of the ruling classes, I am forced to the conclusion that the worst felon brutes we have are in official positions and not in the prisons where they ought to be.

ALL wealth is produced by co-operated labor. A great factory is a pretty example of nicely organized co-operation. Even farm work is co-operative for the tools and clothing are not the farmer's own work. Because the people refuse to co-operate themselves the capitalists do it for them and take the profit. When the people have been taught sufficiently by the capitalists they will co-operate themselves. Then will the workers get all the products and the useless people none. Men will have to do useful work to share in the benefits. Then the workers will be the capitalists.

THERE are lots of people who would be king if the people would permit it, but is that a valid reason that we should have a king and that kingship is good? The fact that lots of people would like to monopolize industries and become millionaires is not a valid reason why the people should uphold a system under which it is possible for a few to do it.

IF you owned a ten-story business house would you permit some man or a company of them to own the elevator in that house? Of course none but a fool would think of such a thing. But is that not just what the owners of a city do when they permit the elevators called the street cars that run up and down their streets to be owned and controlled by a corporation? Are not street cars to a city just what an elevator is to a large building? Do a little thinking, you long-eared mule of a voter.

EASY LESSONS IN SOCIALISM.

ABOUT practicability. If socialism were established and we found that under its operation thousands were driven to suicide, if we found a large portion of the population living in ignorance, squalor and dirt; if we found women driven to prostitution, if we found children being driven to work when they should be in school, if we found dens of vice where the innocent were entrapped and murdered, if we found that officers were bribed, if we found that workmen were shot down like dogs because they asked for enough to eat—I say, if we found these things, would you not at once consider socialism impracticable and decide that it should be abolished? Most assuredly. Well, do we not find these things present with us under the system of competition and private capital today? And are they not the result of the present system? We know this system produces these things. We do not know that socialism will produce them for socialism has not been tried. If your argument would be valid in the case of socialism, and it would be, why is it not valid against the present system? If the effects of the present are practical, please let us try something impracticable for a while and see how it goes. It could not be worse.

A VERY frequent objection to socialism is, that by having the public operate the industries there would be no end of corruption and stealing by the officer from the people.

Which suggests to me: If we cannot trust men whom we select and can control by our votes, how are we to trust the capitalists to operate the industries, whom we do not select and cannot control by our votes? Will they not use the ownership and control to skin the people to get more wealth just as you say the men you vote for would do? Are they not doing it openly, because you have no right to question their methods, the property being theirs to do with as they please? There would be some danger. Now to the capitalists there is none.

But you fail to see that under socialism public officials would be foremen, managers, superintendents, and the like, and would have no more opportunity of stealing than postmasters. There would be nothing left to contractors so that there might be a "stand in" with officials and the public charged many times the cost of what a thing is worth. Nearly, if not quite all, the public corruption comes from the system of contracting out public business to "stand in" friends. Socialism would abolish this by having all work done by the people for the people, the time employed being the cost of a thing.

A READER wants to know just the details of how socialism is to be established. The first thing to do is to get the people to want socialism, which they will when they understand it. That is the FIRST step. In the abolition of chattel slavery or of breaking away from King George, agitators were first and all important. They did not pretend to detail just the methods that would be followed, but they knew if they could get the people to see the matter right that the results would be right. If the change comes in peace it will be by the new desire of the people causing them to elect people to public office who will proceed to have the public engage more and more in business. Every public utility should be taken over and this followed by such industries as are most necessary to the complete operation of them. Thus the public ownership of railroads would require the public to own and operate coal and iron mines because it will be the greatest user of these things. The public will demand that their government sell them the product as cheap as it costs—and this will lead to that principle of government that will permit the people to do for themselves what capitalists only have been furnishing. You will hear more and more about revolution from the old party papers from now on as the only way out of the fix they have gotten the country in. How the thing will be done depends solely on the education of the people. But one thing is certain—the public must engage in business.

CHANGING HUMAN NATURE?

When two or more men are competing for business they will, in the struggle, break the friendship of long years. Their relationship is such that they cannot feel like brothers toward each other. Now let them combine, form a partnership, and see how quickly they will become friends and work for the common fund in which all share! You see the difference is the difference in the relationship between them regarding wealth. They are the same men they were before. Human nature has not changed an iota. It was not necessary to change nature to make them brothers; all that was necessary was to change their property relationship. The partnership did that. Now go on with the principle, make all capital used in commerce public property and you will see just the same change on a great scale in the conduct of men toward each other. Socialism will do that. It is just what socialists demand and demand for just that reason. Under socialism no one will have a special profit by reason of any act he may do. All good work will help the whole, all bad work will injure the whole. All will, therefore, be interested in having only good work done and in not having bad or defective work done. Men cannot hold the real brotherly love feeling to each other under this system of private gain, because their interests conflict. Their interest must be mutual. Socialism will do this by making each and all owners in the capital of the whole nation so that none will compete against another, except for that public approbation which will be given to men for good acts—acts bringing good to all the people. That will bring honor to men such as the world has never yet given men, and it will produce a thousand inventors and discoverers where there is now one. It will not be necessary to offer more "pay," for each will have all he can use of that and more of it would bring no added delight. It does under this system, but would not under socialism. The change there would be just like the change produced by the men going into partnership. As the men forming the partnership would save energy they wasted in numerous rents, capital and other expenses, replacing them with one under better conditions, so socialism would save ALL the wastes of this system and bind humanity into a real brotherhood, not a theoretical one in which they spend most of their time and talents in knifing each other. Rich men are abandoning private capital with its hell of competition and merging their capital into a communism of self-co-operation.

WHAT is the progress you speak about? The Romans considered it progress when they killed their neighbors and took their country. In fact all nations have had no other idea of progress than conquering other people and forcing their own laws, customs and beliefs on them. The dominant idea of the country, however, is that progress means new inventions! That man is fulfilling his divine mission if he will only invent some new contrivance to coin money out of the hides of his fellows. That man's sphere in nature is to make machines! My idea of progress is that condition in which will be developed the greatest possible number of physically and mentally healthy, well-clothed, well-fed, well-housed, well-instructed and entertained men, women and children. Government or no government, religion or no religion, machines or no machines, there is no progress unless this be the goal.

THE person who assumes that socialism means dividing up the property should go and soak his head in a treatise on socialism for an hour or two and let in some sunlight. Socialism is just the opposite of dividing up. It means concentration to the uttermost so that division is impossible. We have division now, and the schemers divide up all that the workers of the world produce. When you hear a fellow talk about dividing up, know that he is ignorant on the subject he talks of. You will always see a smile on the lips of socialists when "dividing up" is mentioned. These ignorant fellows will never convince socialists of their error unless they talk against what socialism is, for the socialist can at once see their ignorance, and no ignorant fellow ever convinced one who knows.

DID you never stop to think that sickness and pain are abnormal conditions —that they are always the result of violations of natural law? Well, they are, and if man were living under right SOCIAL relations he would have none of them. When yellow fever or smallpox or other diseases break out what do you do? Why you people are compelled to clean up the premises, to take greater sanitary precautions and in time you stamp out the disease. Now, if a little cleaning up will drive out those diseases when they have a foothold, would not better, say perfect, sanitary conditions have prevented them from appearing at all? Now when socialism shall be the principle applied to the social contact, the public will build or permit only the most sanitary houses, and the people will live under perfect sanitary conditions. Then why will diseases appear? Then physicians will not draw their pay from the sick, but from the public as honored officials, whose sphere will be to keep the people from getting sick rather than curing them when sick. But if nobody got sick today how would the doctors live? Did you ever think of that? All these wrong relations will be harmonized under socialism.

ARE YOU FOR PROGRESS?

If we admit that the competitive system has done good work in its time, is that any reason why it should continue when better methods have been evolved? The forked stick for a plow, the oxteam for transportation and other similar things did service, but when methods that could bring more pleasure to the world were thought out they were thrown aside. Public ownership of industries have everywhere in every place demonstrated that they are better for the people than private ownership of them. Then why continue the ox team of industry when a better way is pointed out? Why continue a system that slaps profits on every article at every stage of its production when there is a system that will permit you to have the articles without the profit? The profit you make on some article or articles does not balance what you have to pay on all other articles you use. Is it better that you pay ten to twenty cents a gallon for oil than to pay one cent, which has been testified it can be sold at as a public monopoly, just to enable a few men to acquire millions? Are you benefited because these few become enormously rich? And the same with all other articles. I am not blaming the monopolists, because this system compels them to act as they do. But why should you support such a system? Putting it at low estimate, people can produce, on the average, more than $2,500 worth of wealth a year by the use of public capital. Would you not be benefited by that? And do you not want to be benefited? And would not most of your neighbors be likewise benefited by such an income? Why do you get mad at us socialists because we want you to have such an income for yourself and your children after you? Is it something bad—something that will injure them? Would you really be injured by the right to have employment at such a recompense? This is the whole theory of socialism in a nutshell. If you would like it, help us to bring it in. It will cost you nothing to help. You give your vote now to men to do things as they are done; why not give them to men who want them done in a way that you may get what you produce?

UNDER socialism who would do the dirty work? asks a reader. As far as may be, machinery will do it. It will do a great deal that is now done by hand because the cost of machinery is now more considered than humanity. What of dirty work is necessary for the well-being of society, the members of society should do, and do now, in an ignorant, crude way. Volunteers asked for would get the willing workers, or it might be arranged that each able person would be required to serve a certain time in such capacities, as Bellamy dreamed, or shorter hours might be allowed. When no necessary work is looked down on as it is today there will be no stigma attached to it and it will not be shunned as it now is and thrown on the shoulders of such as poverty today compels to accept. Does it seem absurd to you that men cannot be found to do things necessary when we can find men today who will enlist in an army to be made targets of for bullets? Offer a little honor, an empty bauble, to men and they will yield up their lives for the most foolish things today, and men will be honored for good deeds under socialism, even though it soil their hands, and there will be no lack of willing volunteers. There will also come dishonor for such as will not do their part. There will be no trouble in having all necessary work done, and that, too, without having poverty as a task master to force it.

NO WORK, NO PAY.

There be some of you who express great fear that under socialism somebody would get something without working for it. Does it ever occur to you that under the present system many people get something without working for it? In fact, do such people really know what work should get returns and what should not? Bad work, no matter how hard or how assiduously followed, should have nothing, but under the present system it receives the most, while good work is poorly paid. The man who works hard to bribe legislatures, congress and the judiciary accumulates a fortune; the man who works hard to monopolize any necessity of life that he may levy tribute on his fellows is rewarded with wealth and social position. If mere work is the only requisite to reward, these people are entitled to the reward. The counterfeiter, the forger, the robber, the thief—all these work, and some of them exhibit the highest skill—but will anyone assume they should be rewarded because of WORK? The test of reward should be productiveness in good work—work that produces something for the benefit of mankind. And be sure that you know what is good for mankind before passing over the benefits. When you shall have carefully studied the matter you will find, as all philosophers have found, that work spent to get a living through interest, rent or profit is not good work and produces nothing and should have nothing. It is on the same plane with the cunning that elevates one family to a kingship, another to a dukedom, another to a mastery over broad acres, or sugar, or oil, or coal. All belong to the same class and are deserving of the same lack of reward. The people who do the good work of the world, who produce its food, clothing, houses, instruction and entertainment, are entitled to all of these things, while those who do not help produce them by real labor with the one aim of production are not entitled to any of them. Look about you and see which class has these things! You are continually rewarding those who will not work—at least do no good work—and yet express fear that this very thing would be under socialism. Under socialism the social organism could only pay for good work. It is the reverse of this system which pays for bad work or no work. There was a time when people thought they could not get along without a king—that the king kept order and prevented the people from robbing and killing each other; that he protected them with foreign foes; when, in fact, the king was doing all the robbing, was setting them to killing each other and was continually getting them into wars with other peoples. There are people today who are as blind, who believe that they could not get along without capitalists, that the people would sit around and starve if capitalists were not at hand to tell them what to do, and that they would have no work but for the capitalists. One set is just as foolish as the other. Railroads, telegraphs, factories and farms could and would run without capitalists just as the postoffice does, and all that the capitalists draw from the production of society is what ignorance pays to cunning. The employes of all capitalists would do their work as well and just as faithfully if they were paid directly by society (government) as they do when paid indirectly by society through the capitalists who take the greater part of what they produce. Do a little thinking now and then, and you will improve your mind just as exercise improves your muscles.

THE question is often asked if the government employed the idle, how would it pay them. There is no new principle involved. Did you ever stop long enough in your insane scramble for "money" to think how any employer pays his workmen? No, I'll venture you have done nothing of the kind. Let us examine this for a moment, or are you too busy or despairing to listen? Let us take any employer of any number of men and see how he does and see if the same method applied to the government will not answer the oft-asked question. A manufacturer employs a gang (how very appropriate a term, from slaves chained together) of workmen to make shoes. At the end of a week or month these workmen have made shoes to the market price of two or three times their wages. These shoes are sold and the men get their pay. You will notice the employers have not paid the men—the men have made their own pay and paid the employer. It does not alter the case if the shoes are not at once sold, because the shoes are made to meet a demand and that demand is always buying shoes enough to pay wages. Every line of production is exactly like this—even the building of houses and railroads, though it may not at first seem so. Now could not the government sell the product of its workmen to pay its workmen just the same as the private employers? If not, why not? The government, if it would conduct every line of trade, would not need a dollar to pay its employed—it could give them orders on the government store and for these orders they could get at labor cost any article they can now buy with money. What would they need then, with money? All the money paid out is finally converted into food, clothing, rent and mutual pleasures, and if these can be had for the orders to be obtained only by labor in some capacity, money could do no more, and there would be no more use for bonds. The trouble is not that the thing is impracticable or visionary, but the men who rule this nation and all other nations have a

The Appeal's First Home and Working Force, 1895.

"soft snap" at the ruling business and don't want to give it away. Kings are not known for their desire to extend the liberties of the people. If you were in their places instead of being a wage-slave, you would like to keep your fellows as voting cattle to sustain you in your position, perhaps, but you are not the rulers, but the under millions. It will be to your interest to change the condition of employment just as it is to the rulers' interest to maintain the present order.

I AM asked to explain the difference between productive and non-productive labor. Just what percentage of the present labor of the world is non-productive is very hard to define, but a very large percentage of it undoubtedly is. All servants of the rich are non-producers. All armies and navies, all people employed in producing luxuries for the non-producing class are non-producers, though their labor may be of the hardest and the products of their hands of the highest skill. If it would require one store with ten clerks to supply the retail demand of a community that now has ten or fifteen stores, then all the persons engaged in merchandising in that community, except the ten absolutely required under the best economic conditions, are non-producers. This is apparent everywhere. The labor in building many barns for farmers when a scientifically constructed barn would accommodate many of them, the multiplying of farm implements and the labor employed in producing them to a greater degree than would be necessary to conduct farming under one co-operative orderly system, I say that all this excess of labor is non-productive. You will find in a city two and possibly three directories when one would suffice. Under the present system, a man having the monopoly of the directory business would take from the public as much or perhaps more money than two or three, but that does not alter the fact that the labor employed in producing two or three directories, when one is sufficient, is waste. If a city were to publish its own directory and sell it to the public at cost, there would be no incentive for several directories nor for an exorbitant charge for the same. Speaking of printing, it is interesting to note the cost of matter produced at the government printing office. The Congressional Record edition of "Protection or Free Trade," by Henry George, consisting of 111 pages, is printed upon the very best of paper and sold to congressmen at a cost of one cent each and enclosed in a large envelope. There is no place on the market that I could buy that envelope for the price that the government furnishes the envelope, book and all. Now, printers get better pay in the government printing offices than they do in any private establishment, so that this work does not cut down the price of labor, though sold at a price that no private enterprise could compete with. Of course, there is much labor lost in a public printing office from the fact that much matter is printed for which there is no earthly use. It is labor lost when one railroad is paralleled by another, for there is scarcely a community in the United States or the world where a well equipped railroad cannot take care of all the traffic that can be brought to it. It is true that the building of a second road is a benefit to laborers by allowing them to gain something to eat and wear, but that could be better given them out of the earnings of the road, than by hiring them to waste labor and material in another. I might go on multiplying instances *ad infinitum,* but these I think will suffice to show what I mean by non-productive labor.

ONCE upon a time a king was much pleased with the great care bestowed upon, and the wonderful product of the farm of one of his subjects, and he sent for him and told him he wanted all the farmers taught to care for the soil and its fruit as did he. The farmer was a philosopher and he told his king he could have all his kingdom as well planned and planted as his estate, but it would take time. In the first place it would take several years to train up a few, it would take several more for these few to train up more and several generations would pass before enough teachers were educated to begin the instruction of the masses. The king was informed that if he would adopt this course, that while he might not reap much reward while living, that future generations would rise up to bless and honor his name. That coming generations would be born into a world of beauty, love and plenty. But the king was impatient, caring more for immediate gratification and results, and his kingdom went to destruction at a time when it should have been in the zenith of its greatness had the philosopher's advice been taken.

Just so is the condition of the United States. It has reformers and reformers, but for the most part they are like the king, impatient and desire results by a shorter process than they can be obtained. There is one way they can win —and only one way. They must begin the slow process of economic education. They must first create teachers and then open schools. One man who knows the problem is worth hundreds of half educated voters who are liable to ruin a promising crop. See what a Ruskin or a Tolstoi or a Marx has accomplished. Gather as many as you can into your homes, read and discuss books teaching the problem and gradually spread the circles as did the abolitionists and the German socialists. Vote to show your strength, but success is not possible until you have a majority educated and then neither army, navy, judges, ballot box stuffers or other enemies of mankind can prevail against you. Use papers and leaflets freely, raise a fund, be it ever so little, for buying literature. Do this and in ten years the United States will be a co-operative commonwealth. Struggle with a half educated class even if you get the offices, and you will find the fruits of victory turn to ashes.

WHAT is this social system we live under that you ask me to bow down and worship if I am to be accounted a good citizen? Is it something so wonderfully perfect? Does it bring peace, happiness and wisdom to its devotees? Does it provide plenty for its supporters? Does it reward merit and punish demerit? Are the honest and industrious crowned with the product of toil and do the dishonest and useless suffer the pangs of worthlessness? Just the reverse of this seems to me to be true. I see those whose labor has made its bread, hungry, those whose labor has made its raiment, ragged, those who have builded its houses, tenants, those who have builded its railroads, tramping, and those who have made presidents and governors, beggars for crumbs from the table they have spread.

I see the poor taxed and the rich go free. I see the workers reduced to mere wage slaves, hirelings to the vicious, avaricious and corrupt. I see want and ignorance in millions of homes. I see men reduced to mere beasts of burden, so cheap no care is taken whether they receive enough food to exist. I see women and children cooped up like so many hogs gathering fat wealth for the use of their owners. I see the earth as a piece of private property upon which all who live must pay the cunning who have possession. I see the food of the world monopolized by fiends who compel all others to work for them on pain of starvation. I see everywhere cunning, covetousness and avarice housed in palaces, clothed in finest raiment and feasting on the daintiest preparations while the industrious are reduced to menial servants for them. You ask me to endorse a system productive of these enormities on pain of your displeasure. I prefer your displeasure to honor for worshiping such enormities. Our ancestors worshiped at the shrine of any brutal king who could possess himself of the law-making machinery of their land; they bowed ignorant obedience to ignorant and venal customs and superstitions; they were loosed like bloodhounds on any who dared to raise their voice against the system. But that time is passed. A new light is shedding its rays into millions of minds. Too many are disgusted with the present social anarchy and crimes. Too many socialist books and papers have been read despite the care of the millionaires to keep the people in ignorance. Too many people see the present injustice as it is and not as you believe it, for it to last. The real revolution is of ideas and always precedes the final overthrow of a system or dynasty. Men rally around an idea but the work is going on now the effects of which will be noticed in a few years. The people have caught the "how" to stop this criminal system. The nation and state and cities shall monopolize for the equal benefit of a few. Its change is only a matter of sentiment expressed in the ballot box. And until it is so expressed there it is useless to think of any other method.

IF public ownership is not good, let us sell our public roads, streets and alleys to some syndicate and have it fix the terms on which we can use them as they do the railroads. Let us sell the rivers to another syndicate. Let us sell the school houses, court houses, state and national buildings to another syndicate and have it put on its tariff. Public ownership is right or not right. If public ownership will give the people as good or better service than private ownership and for less money (labor) then it is better. The question is simply one of business. The private ownership has proven an abortion. Under it in all nations is poverty and oppression. Those who own the land and machinery squeeze the many who do not own the land and machinery. They want more, more, more. They cut wages, discharge willing workers, bribe city, state and national officers, squander their profits and force the workers to live lives of misery. You never heard of the owners of the public roads, streets, alleys, public buildings or postal system bribing lawmakers, or drawing dividends on watering stock. Had the railroads been public property you would never have heard of the rich and favored riding on passes; you would never have heard of railroad lobbies in your city, state or national assemblies.

Private property is the essence of kingship. It is the mainspring of all corruption, all poverty, all vice, and all disease. It does not make any difference whether you or the majority have not looked at it in this way; it makes no difference whether you deny it; the fact remains there just the same. You may shut your eyes and say it is not true, that something else is the matter and that things will right themselves, but all the same the statement is eternally true that private ownership of monopolies is doing up the masses of all nations, and they are writhing and squirming under the conditions imposed by the present system and will to the end of time—or until they by some means make all the oppressive monopolies public property. You may curse and hang the men who tell you these truths, and swear such are the cause of all your troubles; you may work yourself into a frenzy and believe you are sane, but all the time you will be suffering the effects of your illogical, unnatural ownership, and men of wealth will multiply but men of poverty will multiply a hundred fold faster. You may hug the selfish delusion that you will be one of the wealthy, or being one will remain so, but the whirligig of private property will grind you finer and finer and drop you into the abyss of poverty, your children will be wage-slaves and hirelings who will work, live and have their being just so long as some man can use them to his pleasure or profit —and no longer. You get nothing but disappointment and worry under this system. If you would seek to know what the other system we advocate really is you would be its advocate as are the millions who have studied and investigated.

LET me whisper in your ear a wonderful secret. It would have filled the earth with joy and gladness had it been told the people in the long ago. There would have been no wars, no tyrannous rulers, no crimes, no poverty and but few sorrows and these few tinged with a bright lining. It is what all philosophers sought and the whole world has yearned to realize its effects. It is greater than the philosopher's stone, and why that *ignus fatuus* was sought. This secret is not the discovery of one man, but of many; not in one age, but in all; not in one country, but in every land where the human mind has been capable of serious and right thinking. It has not been kept as a secret—on the contrary every discoverer has tried with his best effort to tell it far and wide, yet to the mass of mankind it is still a secret, as though it had never been discovered. And when I, like the many who have preceded me, tell you this wonderful knowledge, it will still be secret to the most of you who read these lines, for although I shall put it into the simplest, plainest words, words you use every day, you will still be far from comprehending it, or realizing its great, its vital importance. It is this: A nation of busy people, properly directed, can produce by a daily labor of five hours, more wholesome food, more first-class clothing, more excellent houses, and more noble entertainment that the people can consume. If these things be given to each in proportion to the number of days he or she works, all the joys and gladness I have enumerated will naturally follow.

Yes, possibly, you may say, but how is this condition to be brought about? By the product of every man's hands and brain (and I put hand labor advisedly before brain labor) being taken charge of by the whole people (government) and every man going to the whole people (government stores or warehouses) to get whatever he or she needs, presenting certificates of labor for the pay. This system would give no opportunity for the idler to live on interest, rent or profit, and would leave ample means and time for the development of every nature genial to peace—as Shakespeare, Milton, Ruskin, a Michael Angelo, Tintoret or Turner, a Watt, Stephenson or Edison, a Darwin, Humboldt or Agassiz, a Jenny Lind or Patti Rosa. Men and women under those conditions would no longer make private wealth the aim of life, but would seek the honor for good deeds done for all of which they would be adored by a nation of intelligent, happy, progressive people. Great deeds are never done for money, and no great deeds will ever be done while money rules the world, except in rare instances by "peculiar" individuals. Under such conditions what incentive to crime can you conceive? Will you grasp this secret, carry it in your heart, nurture it by your most earnest desire and help propagate it? What a noble thing to live and labor to bring about such a condition.

IMPRACTICAL.

It would be so *impractical* to raise and prepare food for use instead of for profit.

It would be so *impractical* to make clothing for people to wear instead of for profit.

It would be so *impractical* to build houses to live in instead of an income for some landlord.

It would be so *impractical* to build railroads for people to ride on and send goods where needed, instead of for speculation.

It would be so *impractical* to mine coal for people to burn instead of for making coal millionaires.

It would be so *impractical* to refine oil for use instead of profit for the Standard Oil tyrants.

It would be so *impractical* to build theatres and opera houses for people to enjoy, instead of for the profit of a few schemers.

It would be so *impractical* to construct street cars, water works, gas and electric plants for the people to enjoy, instead of for a few to get wealthy on.

So wonderfully, so ridiculously impracticable are any such suggestions that the foolhardy advocates of such wild, visionary, utopian ideas are considered insane, while those who are being robbed by the present *practical* system are so *very very* sane! And man is said to be endowed with reason! He believes the lies told him by those who are robbing him into poverty and ignorance, but has only loathing for those who advocate a system that would yield peace, plenty and pleasure to all. The new system would not benefit any of its advocates an iota more than it would benefit any other man or woman in the land. There are no hard or soft jobs in the new order, but honest work is demanded of everyone if that one eats.

THE STREET CAR GRIPMAN.

Said I to a street car gripman the other day: "Don't you working people get tired of slaving for a corporation for the miserable pay you get?"

"Yes; it is hard work and poor pay, but we have to work for somebody."

"Yes, so all you laboring people are taught to think, but the truth is otherwise. Your masters, I see by the daily press, make a profit of sixty to seventy thousand dollars a month, besides the fat salaries of its chief directors. Now, do you not see that either the fares ought to be reduced to the people or your wages raised?"

Said he: "The company must have a profit. They would not employ us if they could not make a profit."

"Yes, so you think, but you are not so well paid as the postal employes, and I am sure no company is making a profit off them. All the people pay for stamps and it is paid to the employes, except that part paid the railroads; there is no part of the receipts taken to pay dividends on honest or dishonest stock, or honest or dishonest bonds, or fancy prices to some officers and starvation prices to some employes as is the case with this street car company. Your hours are not so favorable to you as postal employes' and your job is not so secure to you. You dare not organize a union, and have no liberty of voting as you please, except you vote one of the old party tickets. The postal employes are nearly all organized and get favorable legislation."

Said he: "All you say is about a fact, but the postoffice is a government business."

"Yes, and these street railroads would be city business if you laboring people would vote for men who want the city to own them, and then you would stand in the same relation to the street car department that the postal clerks do to the postal department. You could organize then and your vote for aldermen and mayor would protect you. Now your vote is not worth anything to you, because the men you vote for have little or nothing to do with your pay or treatment. Then the council would regulate your wages, and they would have no interest but justice in adjusting them, as they now adjust the pay of policemen, firemen and other city employes. Now, the street car company can put in its purse all they can cut your wages or lengthen your hours."

Said he: "I think most of us want better conditions, but the men we vote for promise well before the election and then sell us out."

Look at the globe we call our earth. It is our mother, and it has on it, and in it, the elements with which every legitimate desire of every man, woman and child can be satisfied to the uttermost. Only one thing is required of man and it will make him happy. The earth will not give up these blessings to the children of men except they *labor* —labor with hands and brains. Not one of these but both of these must be applied. The brain can no more cozzen mother earth out of a grain of pleasure without the hands of labor, than the hands can without any brain connected with them. That is the grand test of useful labor. Whenever you see some man getting a living by his "Great brain power," and doing nothing useful with his hands, he is not swindling mother earth—he is swindling some worker or workers out of a part of what they gain by labor on mother earth. No man, no matter what his mental accomplishments, can *think* a dinner into being— it takes work and intelligence to do that. If he gets a dinner it is by deceiving some one who has produced the dinner —trading sophistry and lies for his dinner. You can't lie to mother earth.

She gives nothing up except it first be earned. Labor you must, or of her you cannot get your dinner. Not so much as a drop of water from her surface can you get except physical exertion necessary to lift it be made. In her storehouses are food for billions, clothing for billions, houses for billions, instruction and entertainment for billions—all to be had for labor. All these have been enjoyed by a few without labor, under the pretext that they were entitled to them because they were kings, nobles, priests, capitalists, soldiers and landlords, and the silly millions whose labor had wrested these things from earth, supplied these useless drones with the best they produced and took the leavings for themselves. The idle parasites have been the cause of every war, every crime and all the poverty that has ever visited the human race. Is it not time, in this closing of the XIX century, that the people throw off the burden of maintaining these drones and by a public ownership of the earth and the fullness thereof leave no avenue by which they may get their dinner except by producing its value in absolute wealth? They have been maintained under false pretenses long enough.

You know I have often said that this social anarchy, miscalled civilization gives peace and pleasure to neither the rich nor poor—that the rich are just as miserable in mind as the poor. In fact, I believe that with few exceptions they suffer more, and not infrequently we read of their suicide, even while surrounded with plenty, to get away from the intense struggle for supremacy with possible failure and want staring them in the face. An instance in point came under my observation a few days ago. Talking with an old friend who was considered quite wealthy four or five years ago, but who told me he was carrying a heavy financial load, we drifted into a discussion of the hopes and aims of socialism, and how it would bring a boon of comfort and peace to the rich as well as to the poor. He repeated to me in part a conversation he had with one of the foremost bankers and capitalists in the country. I know the party and know he is quoted at fifteen millions. My friend asked him if he was going on a vacation this year. "No, the governess and children are going to the seashore, but I cannot spare the time." Think of it—a man worth millions who could not leave his affairs long enough to take a rest for fear the fabric he had built would tumble down! What glorious satisfaction is wealth! And the man is not a miserly, mean man, either. He dared not leave his affairs. This conversation was in the rich man's counting house. He walked the floor as they talked. Coming up before my friend he said: "If I could be guaranteed against want I would gladly lay down all I have gathered—give it up." There you have it—there is no happiness in wealth. It is a burden and curse. For it men commit all crimes, live a life of toil and struggle and care—just to find or feel sure of that one thing— "guarantee against want"—which a socialist system would guarantee to every citizen who would do two or three months' useful labor in a year. And for six months' labor one could enjoy more of pleasure, more of travel, more of all that makes life worth living than this fifteen-millionaire ever has or ever will enjoy—and he is not sure that his children will not beg bread. People oppose socialism because they do not know what it is. But socialism is of more worth as a legacy to children than a million dollars under this system.

Did you ever hear of any watered stock in the postal system? Nit.

Did you ever hear of any bonds, stocks or mortgages connected with it? Nit.

Did you ever hear of any princely salaries or useless officials? Nit.

Did you ever hear of any official using the system for his private pleasure or profit without paying postage like other citizens? Nit.

Did you ever hear of a postoffice lobby in city council, state legislature or congress clamoring for greater privileges or bribing officials? Nit.

Did you ever hear any talk about the business not paying an interest on the investment in building, machinery, etc.? Nit.

Isn't it about the only thing in the land where the investment is not expected to pay an interest? YOU bet.

All business can be so conducted, and no thought of interest, rent or profit will ever enter the mind of the people engaged in it. When a building is built, it will be for use and no thought of rent will be connected with it any more than there is with the rent of a public building erected for a postoffice. It will be thus under socialism.

ANYTHING that is right in theory is right in practice. Anything wrong in theory is wrong in practice. People have not been taught to comprehend these facts. Now what is right and what is wrong depends upon the results desired. If you build a clock that will not keep time, but will make a ribbon the thing is wrong—it does not produce the results you seek. You have the wrong theory and have wrong results. But if the object you sought was ribbons it would be constructed on the right theory, because it produced what you sought. In this light of reason let us analyze the present theory of society, private ownership of property with its effects of competition, and see if it is right in producing the effects or product that we seek. If we seek strife, deception, fraud, embezzlement, perjury, forgery, theft, robbery, suicide, murder, war, poverty, hunger and ignorance—I say if these are the products we seek, then the present social and political theory we are following is perfectly right, for these are the results. But if we desire other and opposite results; if we desire peace, plenty and pleasure, then the present theory is all wrong. The question of right or wrong depends on which of these results we want. If we desire peace, plenty and pleasure we will have to construct society on another theory. There are only two theories regarding wealth and its holding—it must be either private property or public property. We have the effect of private property, effects present in every nation in every age, regardless of the laws governing it. If we like them, then no change is needed. If we want other results we must apply public ownership—socialism. There is no other road. Socialism is a theory that will produce peace, plenty and pleasure. If you want these things, vote the Socialist ticket and help build up a party to apply socialism.

SOCIALISM would not abolish all private property. Communism would do that. Socialism would have all the people own everything that is used to produce wealth—land and machinery. It means the employment of each individual, according to his ability, by all the people—or as we term it, government. The creation of the labor so employed belongs to all the people, but the order, money or pay that I would get would buy back all I produced or its equivalent of what others produced. When so bought it becomes my private property, but I could not buy land, or machinery—nor would I want to, for I could get the use of it without buying.

PLAIN TALKS TO WORKING MEN.

So you think that politics has nothing to do with your wages or chance of getting employment, or your debts or poverty, eh? The banker tells you so. The politician tells you so. The monopolist tells you so. The people who live well and do nothing tell you so. Isn't it funny that all of these people are all of one mind? All these people live off of somebody. Do you know who that somebody is? All these people are very anxious about the elections. Do you ever ask yourself why? If politics has nothing to do with you why are you so interested? Do you think they are fools to spend their time and money on something there is nothing in for them? And if there is something in it for them, who pays that something? Why can't you see a little bit under the surface? Have they trained you like a soldier so you can't think but obey orders? Why are they so anxious that you don't vote with the Socialists? Why all this solicitude? Politics has everything to do with your wages and employment. It can render millions of you idle so you will have to work cheap, or it can have all of you busy getting big wages. They don't want you to find this out. They want you for a voting machine to help them live in luxury and power. And you've been doing it.

WHY should one man have more pay than another, for labor? Is it because one needs five or ten times as much food, or five or ten times as much clothing, or five or ten times as much house or pleasure? Is this the reason one should have five or ten times as much pay? If one don't need these more than another, why should he be allowed to take them? Why do the poor, who want and NEED an equal share of pay for labor, vote for a system that pays them dog's crumbs and gives to idlers the banquet?

ONCE upon a time there was a great howl about "negro equality" in this land. But you hardly ever see a gang of workmen that these same fellows are not on working equality and the white fellows feel lucky to get work on these terms. Strange things happen in a few years. This equality don't reach the rich. The poor whites voted themselves and the colored people both to their present poverty stricken conditions.

Workman—Could you advance me a week's pay?

Boss—No, sir.

Workman—Why ever since I have worked for you I have been advancing my labor before being paid, thus enabling you to carry on your business.

Boss—That cuts no figure. *You* ought to be thankful that you are permitted to work for ME. But what do you want with the money?

Workman—My daughter is very sick and I have no money to buy medicine.

Boss—Sorry, but times are hard—hard, sir. I can't give any money until your week is up. My daughter is going to give a ball tomorrow evening and it will take several thousand dollars to cover expenses.

IT matters not what your politics or religion, you and I desire the same things in this life. Let me prove it to you while you shall be the judge and the jury. You want the best of food, prepared in the best manner, do you not? So do I. You want the best of clothing, made in the best manner, do you not? So do I. You want to live in as good a house as any other citizen and have it furnished as well, do you not? So do I. You want time and means for enjoying the best instruction and the highest entertainment possible, do you not? So do I. This being true, and I am sure it is, why this difference between us? Why do we look with suspicion on each other and vote against each other, and feel that we are enemies of each other? (I do not feel that way toward you.) But you Democrats and Republicans feel that way toward each other and toward the Socialists, if I can judge from your talk and actions. Yet all of you want the same things I have mentioned. And beyond these you want the assurance that you and your children after you may always have these things and every action of your life has for its object the attainment of these things. Now, if you have followed me along these lines, let us reason a little further. Are you afraid to reason? I hope not. I hope you are not afraid of the words another shall write or the sounds which another shall utter. Why should you fear to let your eyes rest on a few letters arranged in any manner? Can such letters tear your flesh? They cannot affect your mind unless you are willing.

So they can do you no harm either physically or mentally. You need not obey them unless your reason tells you they are good. And that is what you are doing all the time, with whatever words, printed or written, that you come across. Going back to the first proposition: All of us desire the same thing —the best of food, clothing, shelter, instruction and entertainment—each according to his tastes. Now, are you getting them? That is the main point. If you are, you have nothing to wish—you must be completely satisfied and happy. But if you are not, do you think you ever will be by continuing as you have? Are the prospects brighter day by day? With all the years in which the Democrats and Republicans have run this country, have they not had time enough to arrange affairs and give every citizen these things, if they knew how or wanted to? Are not both parties just the same? Are not conditions just alike in Democratic or Republican states? What gives you hope that they will make things different from what they have been giving you? We Socialists have been either Democrats or Republicans. We have looked carefully into the question and have come to the conclusion that a change of SYSTEM must be had before all of us can realize the very things that we desire. Five thousand years of private ownership has never given the people of a single nation the things that they really longed for. Now, has it? If not, why still cling to the delusion that it can be realized by pursuing the same old methods? Change must come and why not make it now and enjoy life instead of the present disgusting and irritating worry and uncertainty? After you have examined into the Socialist solution and have convinced yourself that it will not do for us what we desire to have done, then you can come to us and show wherein we are mistaken, and between us we may be able to find some method by which humanity may be able to realize its highest ideal. Now, isn't that fair? What more could you ask? As you are, you have no remedy. You are traveling the same old road that has been traveled so many centuries without producing happiness and brotherhood for the human family. We desire to take another road. Come with us.

You are not going to get something for nothing and get it honestly. Neither are you going to get something for work that in itself produces nothing and get that something honestly. You must produce something yourself, or aid in its production at some stage to be entitled to something honestly. The teacher who produced useful knowledge in a child or a man is a producer, but if it is base ideas he teaches he is not a producer, but a destroyer and is entitled to no rewards, but punishment. Work does not entitle a man to reward unless it be good work. All useless or ill-directed labor is criminal.

Suppose the working people had made twice or thrice the food and clothing and houses and machinery in the last few years would they be any better off today? Not a bit of it. They would not have received any more wages. Do railroad men receive any more wages for hauling a train of thirty heavily loaded cars than they do for half the number of empty ones? The trouble with the present deplorable condition of millions starving and freezing is not that the workers have not produced

The Appeal's Second Home, 1899-1902.

enough, but that they have produced too rapidly for the wages received. The truth is, that the task master, wage-slavers, have taken so nearly all the products of labor just because under the system they can, that what has been paid in wages or for crops will not keep soul and body of the working people together. Had the workers lived like Chinamen, a condition they are nearing, it would be just the same, for then wages would have been reduced to that level. The working people must capture the law making machinery and by the state employ themselves and do away with the speculating class. Then all will be well.

CAPITALISTS do not furnish working people employment. The demand of the public for goods makes employment possible. All the capitalists do is to prevent the working people from working until they agree (for wages) to give the capitalists (for the use of machinery which had been stolen from the workers) most of what is produced. The workers furnish the employers a living, but the employers never furnish the workers a living. So long as a majority of workers are fools enough to believe this lie of capitalists (which is on a par with the lie about the divine right of kings) they will be living like slaves while keeping up a lot of slick drones in luxury. But I am not condemning the drones. So long as the workers have no more sense that to support the capitalistic system they are fit only for work slaves, while their masters live like kings on their toil.

THE NEGRO AND SOCIALISM.

Socialism will solve the race question, and that, too, without a single reference to race and without denying to any person a single right accorded any other person. It will be done in just the way the government or society now employs colored soldiers or provides schools for them separate from the whites. Take, for instance, some great factory. The workers will make the regulations, governing the industry. It would require a majority of the workers to consent to the employment of colored, Chinese, or any other race in that particular factory, a consent not likely to be given. As every citizen would have the right of employment, a rejection of any race would necessitate the erection of a plant of that or some other character in which such colored citizens would be separated from the whites and the whites from the colored people, one not more than the other. The colored race would have the same right to reject or accept the association of whites. It would be to the interest of all to have the colored race furnished with the same good machinery to work with and the same good homes and schools and everything, as the result of their labor would be a matter of interest to all. Thus they would live as well as the whites and have every surrounding to develop and unfold them that could be placed about them. There would be communities or sections of blacks, of Chinese, or of any other races and nationalities, if there were such citizens. You might fear that such guarantee of employment and capital by the public would result in flooding this country with the hordes from other lands. Yes, if a majority of the people here should vote to admit them. But that is not likely. You see the public would own all the land, machinery and means of exchange, and no one could find a place to work, except the majority should make regulations admitting them. They come in now by the millions, with or without your consent, because the private owners of industries can hire them cheaper than you want to work for. You would need no anti-Chinese laws and other farces then. No, Chinamen might come, but Chinamen would not be able to work and live here without your consent. Thus you see that private ownership of industries mixes up the races, reducing blacks, whites and yellows to a common level, while socialism would separate the races and lift them all to the highest level of which each were capable. It would do this without denying one any right possessed by another, without denying employment to any class, and without permitting any to take profit off another. All the hell you see in the fields of industry today, all the riots, strikes and threatened revolution are the results of private ownership, where should be public ownership. All is the result of one set trying to squeeze profit out of the other in some industry. When you get wise you will abolish this hell and institute a heaven. But you will have to suffer a little longer before your dulled perception will see the cause of your misery.

THE time is coming, if not already here, when there will be no more masters of trades. No one would be foolish enough to learn the shoemaking trade today, for the factory has usurped that field. Any unskilled worker can go into a shoe factory and learn to attend one of the numerous machines in a few days and help to put out shoes, yet he would not be able to make a pair of shoes. Clothing is being made in the same way. All food products are fast falling under the same condition. Machines for the production of these things are made in the same way. Doctors and pharmacists and lawyers will be thicker than the people who can use them, and these will not be more independent than the machine tenders. What are you going to do with your sons and daughters? What trade or profession can you give them that will insure them a living? Learn the printing business? Why, the machines can set type at ten cents a thousand, and seven thousand is a good day's work for a *printer* (not a machine operator). And a new machine is promised that will set type at one cent a thousand. Everything in the business is the same way and thousands of good workmen are now idle and tramping in search of work. It is the same in all lines. Great farms will produce products cheaper than a little farmer can hope to, and the little fellow will be out of business as was the shoemaker and the printer. Turn which way you will and you will meet just this condition. If you can find a ray of hope in the future for the masses of the oncoming generation you can see more than I can—you are an optimist indeed, but without reason.

A WORKING man wants to know if the American people, when they get socialism, will have to get up to the ringing of bells or a municipal whistle. Great heavens, man! Come with me to the mines of Pennsylvania or the mills of New England. I will show you where the bells ring the workers to bed at 9 p. m., or they will be discharged. I can show you thousands of men, women and little children rushing to work early in the morning at the sound of bells and whistles, and leaving at night with the same accompaniment. I can show you hundreds who lose their chance to earn a living because they were unable to get to work on the exact moment. Most of these people would welcome socialism, my friend. Do you know what the ringing of the bell of a public factory or the tooting of a "municipal whistle" would mean? It would mean no child labor; it would mean wages for both man and woman sufficient to support them on the best that can be produced; it would mean short hours and the living of workers in desirable localities in country or city, and not in crowded tenement hells; it would mean no more forcing of our sisters and daughters into prostitution because of insufficient wages; it would mean that the public, being the consumers of what they themselves produced, would no longer be poverty-forced to eat adulterated food, wear shoddy clothes or live in ramshackle and unhealthy buildings. And when you hear the municipal whistle or socialist bell at the close of work you will see no half-starved, ill-clothed and tired out wage slaves swarming to the holes they call "home." It will not be at night, with no time to do other than to tumble weary and hopeless into their wretched couches. When the publicly owned industry closes for the day it will be early in the afternoon. There will be public theaters, concerts, libraries, gymnasiums, lectures. There will be enjoyment, happiness, laughter, and they will go to their wholesome, healthy supper in bright homes, a happy people, bright, laughing children, and fathers and mothers no longer tormented with the fear of a poverty-stricken future. The "municipal whistle" and the "socialist bell"! Let us have them. They will be far better than the privately owned whistle and bell that now drives us, whether or no, to ill-paid, exhausting labor that degrades the workers, dulls conscience and morality, and enriches only the few private owners and slave drivers. When the "municipal whistle" and the "ringing of socialist bells" are heard, then also will be heard the joyous cries of an uplifted humanity and the triumphant song of reënthroned justice.

You ought to join the army. It is a nice place. You get feed and covering and kicks. If you do not black the officers' shoes and make yourself a debased servant for the men(?) with straps on their clothes, you are put under arrest and then kicked and dragged by the heels for two blocks to be tried for insubordination. If you complain, a big brute will jab a sword in you while you are a prisoner and helpless. If any of the thefts or brutality of the officers are hinted at by an underling, such underling will have a hard time of it. All the privates in the army know this. It is a great thing to have an army. All tyrannies need them. Nice place for pets of the leading families. The officers are the reliance of the rich. So they are in Europe. Over there only the members of the noble families are allowed to be officers. The officers order; the common herd who do the soldier act are to obey. It would not be safe to allow plebeians to officer the men. They might take a notion to fight for the people instead of the tyrants. So in this country. The army is officered by overbearing brutes. Boys, join the army and fight for the rich.

WHEN a corporation fines an employe for infraction of its rules, it usurps the powers of civil government—legislative, judicial and executive. That is just what constitutes absolute monarchy. But the poor wage slave, laboring under the delusion that he is a free man in a free country, votes to perpetuate the rule of employers. He is taught to fear socialism, because his masters want him to fear it and not read what it is. He remains a slave unconscious of his condition.

WHAT idiocy there is in many of our customs and ideas. Take that elegantly attired man over there—a useless ornament to society. He would not touch the hand of the cook or waiter, but he will eat that which their hands have been manipulating! He would not recognize the poor sweaters who have made his clothing, but will wear them with a strut! He would not associate with the workers who built his palace, but will show it to his friends with pride! He would be disgraced to recognize the artists who delight him on the stage! In other words, it is degrading to wash clothes but respectable to dirty them! Degrading to cook food but respectable to eat it! Degrading to work at house-building but respectable to occupy houses. Really, we have no classes!

"TURN down the light a little, John; we burn too much." And this is the way the poor families are economizing, and deny themselves those necessities of which nature has produced an abundance, because a few robber operators have persuaded the people that they own these products of Nature. Shame on a degraded people who will go on voting to support a system that robs them of the necessities of life. So long as you do the schemers will gladly take it, and you will be their slaves and menials.

HARD times? What do you mean when you say the times are hard? Did you ever try to form a picture in your mind about what hard times does mean? The times are not hard. This particular portion of the infinity of time is not perceptibly different from any other period. It has brought the seasons in regular order, its sunshine and showers, its harvests of all that could happify mankind. Nature has yielded increased return for every hour of toil—more of the good things to eat, drink, wear, shelter, amuse and instruct. Then if this be true times are not hard. The fault lies with men's action toward each other. A few men have persuaded the ignorant many to agree to give these few an ever-increasing amount of what they produce, until the amount has become so great that the producers are retaining not enough to live on, while the few are surfeiting in superabundance. They have allowed themselves to be swindled in the exchange of their handiwork for that of others they wanted. They have permitted the few who have the railroads and commerce to take the greater part of all they create to convey it to another place where wanted and bring back things they desire in exchange. No, times are not hard—they are bounteous to the fullest. But when people let others take from them all they create for merely handling it, they will assuredly be in want and despair.

WHAT hollow mockery the p h r a s e that every man in America is a king! Great and noble kings you are, going from place to place humbly begging a chance to serve your masters who have robbed you of your rights. Shame on such flunkeys — ignorant menials, who know not your God-given rights to anywhere apply your labor in producing and exchanging products unhindered by tribute.

DID you ever notice a man robbing a hive of bees, while the bees flew about him in swarms unable to penetrate his shield? If the man is "civilized" he does not take all the honey, as the bees would starve and thus he would be unable to gather honey in the future.

Did you ever notice men robbing a nation of people, while the people flew about in desperation unable to penetrate their shields of law? If the robbers are "civilized," they do not take everything the people have, as the people would starve, and thus the robbers would be unable to gather wealth in the future.

The two cases are just as similar as the above paragraphs. The man does nothing to produce the honey; the robber barons and trusts do nothing to produce the wealth they hold. They use one set of men to rob all the other workers. They do not work except to scheme how they may rob to the best advantage. If the toiling millions were not blinded by prejudice, this state of affairs would long ago have ceased.

WHAT sight can be more pathetic than to see an old, broken-down man trying to compete with vigorous manhood for a living for himself and family? After forty years of toil, having produced by his labor enough to keep half a dozen families, he finds himself poor and dependent in his old age! Robbed of his earnings through monopoly, as fast as he created it, his life has been one continual drudge, with nothing but the poorhouse or private charity as a reward. Under a just system he could years ago have ceased to work, and spent his declining years in peace and plenty, respected and honored for a useful, industrious life. For the sake of your old father and mother, for your own declining years, vote out this robber system.

LABOR has created all the capital of the world, yet laborers have no capital. They are as easily plucked as children. To take from them is like stealing from a blind man. But every man who sets up a carriage and servants has been doing it. Some poor, toiling animal in human form, or many of them, has been "touched" to enable an idler to set up his style. The workers are so blind that, although one of them has worked every day since childhood, has never enjoyed the luxury of the least extravagance, he can see some man, his neighbor, whom he knows has never done a day's real labor, ride by in the greatest style, and not know it is the unpaid labor of such men as himself that enables the idler to so live in luxury. He is taught to vote some ticket, and the men who steal his intelligence also take his purse. Poor laborers, you have for years voted your wealth into the hands of the Goulds, Vanderbilts, Carnegies, Depews and all the lesser fleecers down to the candidate for constable. Intelligence would make you free. Your crime is ignorance and your present condition is the punishment you have received by order of that Eternal Court that is higher than man-made statutes or constitutions.

OF course you have been in the cities, unless you are one of the poor serfs tied to the soil by poverty just as fast as by the old feudal laws. Did you ever stop on a prominent corner and watch the surging crowds, well-dressed idlers, the 'busses, street cars, carriages? Did you ever ask yourself how all these people live? They produce nothing to eat, wear or drink, nor do they build houses. What do they do for the distant farmer for the meat, bread, wool, cotton, etc., they consume? What do they do for the working man who render these ready for their consumption? Of what use to humanity is all the whirl and bustle, the rushing to and fro? If an American stood in St. Petersburg and saw these things, he could be easily shown that they were supported by royal favors, directly or indirectly, taken from the great mass of workers, but he cannot see that here it is just the same. He remains blind to the deception and fraud by which these leeches live here. He has grown up under it, just as the dupes of Russians have, and does not see the iniquity of it. Whenever you see men living in luxury without producing something, you ought to know that they are eating and living on the toil of others without returning an equivalent. That they pay more money for what they get does not alter it—they do not give an equivalent for the money.

SAY, John. I mean you workingman in the humble walks or toils of life, who by virtue of your station are hardly entitled to the appellation of "Mr." I say, John, are you really satisfied with your occupation, your pay and your surroundings? Is your work of that agreeable nature that makes it a pleasure—for you know that work is not necessarily unpleasant. For instance, I love my work, and prefer to do it than to be idle. Is your pay all you could wish it? And is your home such as is conducive to pleasure and rest? Now, don't think I mean that I am trying to compare your condition with no work or a fabulous income or a life in a palace with servants, but with that condition that the willing labor of men should entitle them to. Do you think you are getting all you deserve? To think requires that you exercise your mind. The class who employ you in mine or shop do not consider you have a mind, and by the way you have wasted your life to produce wealth of which they got the greatest benefit you have not given much evidence of using it. But think. If you are not satisfied with your work, your pay and your surroundings, if you are not able to give your children the advantage that will be good for them, is it not time that you were inquiring why you are so situated? If working for other people or corporations has afforded you only a mean existence, is it not time to work for yourself awhile? And as you have no capital, and as your class has none, why not by a united vote use your government which has control of all property of all people to furnish you employment and give each of you all the value of your labor, deducting nothing for capital, dividends, interest, lawyers, lobbies, bonds and thousands of leaks that now turn your products into the hands of those who do no needed function in production? Then you will be your own capitalist, your own employer, your own employe. Suppose that the coal in Pennsylvania were mined in this way and transported in the same manner. The miners get 75 cents a ton and the railroad employes get 25 cents a ton. It is sold for $4.50. If the government did this business and sold the coal at $4.50 the miners would get $3.00 a ton for mining and the railroad men would get six times their present wages. This will apply to every shop and factory in the land. If you will think, John, and get your fellow workingmen to think, you can live better and have better conditions for your children. True, under this system there could be no millionaires, but I think you could get on well enough without them. Think, John, think!

WORK, WAGES AND SLAVERY.
A BIT O' SLAVERY.

If the slave master had no right to live in comfort and pleasure off the profit derived from the labor of his black slaves, then on the same logic the master today has no right to live by profit off the labor of white and black wage-slaves. The present system is better for the masters and worse for the workers. I could today get thousands of workers if I would furnish them a cabin, food and clothes. I wouldn't have to buy them. They would come and fight and even kill each other to work on terms like the black slaves were released from. The white races are taught they are free. They believe the lie, and go about in hunger, misery and woe, believing they are free. They are thankful to work for enough to keep from starving, and give the employer all the balance. The slaves were better fed than the average white laborer, and were not worked so hard—or at such dangerous vocations. They were too valuable! White men are not so valuable. They cost nothing and the supply is unlimited—in fact, they are pests like grasshoppers that swarm about places where capitalists permit slaves to work for their food until they overrun the places and have to be kept out by high fences and guards at the gate! To such a woeful condition have the working people been reduced by wage-slavery, by "freedom of contract," which is free for the boss, but not the worker. All the poor dupes are afraid of socialism! Afraid to read it! They still take advice from their bosses as to what they ought to read. When one human being makes a profit off another that is slavery. We have slavery today in its most degraded and last form—so horrible that the slaves commit suicide to escape its horrors, a thing chattel slaves never did. Socialism would abolish slavery and give to each all he produced. That is why capitalists oppose it.

THE employer is the task master. He must get all he can out of his wage-slaves, just as did the chattel slave-master. The employes have no interest in the character or product of their labor, any more than the plantation slave. It matters not to him what the profit or losses. If the losses shut down the shops, then the money that kept up that business is spent by the people in some other channel that will employ about the same number. No one is employed to produce goods that people have no money to buy, and the people spend all the money they get. The poor slaves are happy if they can find a master—feel they are lucky and never once suspect the cheat being played on them in the name of freedom. Employers crush each other out just as hungry, idle workmen competing for a job crush each other.

EVER PRESENT BUT INVISIBLE SLAVES.

When I buy, or want to buy, a house or farm or any other property that I do not want to occupy or use personally, it would seem that it was these that I wanted, but a little analysis will show that such is not the case. Let us suppose that I expect that the property will pay a net income of $30 a month, for if there were nothing in it I should not want to buy it, unless to personally use it. Now what I really buy is not the house, but a human slave represented by its income, a slave capable of producing a dollar's worth of service a day and who boards and keeps himself and requires no attention. The great advantage of such a slave is that he or she is ever present, but not visible. My house may be in Colorado, its occupants may know nothing of my existence, yet this slave will serve the railroad company to carry me to New York, will serve the street car monopoly to carry me to the city, will then serve the theater to pay for my box, serves the hotel man to pay for my bill, serves the merchant to pay for my purchases, and thus pays all my bills, according to the number of such slaves I can buy. It is the invisible but ever-present slave that I buy when I buy the house, bonds or other income property. This system of slavery is much better than the other, as the poor slaves are totally unconscious of their slavery and never see their real master. In the old crude form of personal slavery you could have only service as the limited skill of your particular slave could render, but this system of slavery will instantly transform itself into any skill or any place at your wish. And these slaves never protest, but esteem it a great favor to serve you, because they do not see the cheat. It is this phase of property that gives it the value it has, and without which the finest unoccupied lands in the United States would have no more value than they have in Central Africa. Another feature of this slavery is that these invisible slaves will furnish you the money to buy more houses or printing presses or bonds so you can buy more slaves. In other words, they furnish the means to buy themselves and their children into helpless servitude. They furnish the means to hire themselves to act as soldiers and officers to c o m p e l obedience to this form of slavery. These invisible slaves built the palaces for the rich and occupy the hovels and consider themselves lucky to be permitted to serve their masters whom they never see. It is because of this covered up character of the present slavery that it is so hard to dislodge, for few of either of the masters or men realize its true character, else it would not be tolerated for a month. This system will last until the majority realize that service for service, time for time, is the only just method of human association.

DURING the anti-slavery agitation, the defenders of the "peculiar" institution went through the mails and took out and destroyed all copies of Lloyd Garrison's paper, "The Liberator," they could find. The Georgia legislature offered a reward of $5,000 for his capture and demanded of the state of Massachusetts that the incendiary paper be suppressed and the editor arrested with or without law. This is what men did to maintain one form of property—that in chattel slaves. But their system was wrong because it had ill for its effects, and it was doomed as soon as it could be brought to the attention of men. The present system of private ownership is wrong for the very same reason, its effects are destructive, and it, too, is doomed. Its upholders will do even viler things than did the owners of chattel slavery—but it will not perpetuate the villainy of private ownership that really means the ownership of men and women today more effectually than was the ownership of the bodies of the black slaves. It is one of the most interesting things in the history of the country, this struggle of Garrison to print a paper and by tongue and pen arouse the nation to the enormity of the custom. Socialism today is gaining adherents faster than did the anti-slavery movement. Its victory is as sure as the stars in their courses. Organize, organize, organize.

The laborers of this nation, and all other nations, in this century and all other centuries, feed themselves and the rich, clothe themselves and the rich, house themselves and the rich, and furnish all the servants and luxury and finery for the rich. They are too ignorant to make laws that will enable them to retain their wealth and enjoy it themselves. They fall as easy dupes to the schemer today as do the savage of Africa who trades his ivory for glass beads. By those who live off their toil, in state and church and trade, they have been trained as mere serfs that they are, and tickled by being told they are free men, while they furnish more wealth for their masters than any former methods of servitude of which history gives an account. They go in patches and rags and live in shanties or three or four-room "cottages" or in dingy halls in big buildings, and imagine they have all the rights and privileges they are entitled to Never were more degraded slaves than the millions of hard working people in this the closing of the XIXth century. Mental slaves to a colossal lie.

SIXTEEN black slaves worked on a plantation for the old master for many years. They were born on the old plantation, as were their children; as a rule they had plenty to eat, comfortable clothing, a cabin, and they had their days of rest, their holidays, their songs and dances, and no care for the morrow, or the crop, or the markets, disturbed their rest. They had but one master, and that master took more care of them than anything else he owned. When these slaves passed off the scenes of life they left no personal wealth, they left no debts, no wife or children in want or starvation. Their master was richer by what they had created above what they consumed. They came with nothing and went with nothing, and their life had existed for the pleasure of the master.

Now take sixteen white wage slaves and make the comparison along the same lines and see which is the worse. They are born everywhere; as a rule, they do not have plenty to eat, have the poorest of clothing and live in worse quarters than ever slave did. Their days of rest are only struggles to find work, their holidays are carousals that do not as a rule ennoble them, they often dance for misery, but seldom for joy, and the morrow is only a gloomy repetition of yesterday. They have many masters, each of them more exacting, more cruel and more careless than was ever slaves' master. No one cares where they live, how they live, or if they live at all. When these wage slaves pass off the scenes of life they leave no personal wealth, they leave debts, they leave wives and children in danger of want and starvation. Their employers are richer by what they have created above their keeping. They came into the world with nothing and they leave it with nothing, and their whole life has been for the sole pleasure and profit of their employer. Chattel slavery was not right, but wage slavery is far worse.

If other men who own the shop or field you work in, the house you live in, the store you deal at, and regulate the hours of your labor, the price of the goods you buy and the rate of wages you receive—and they do—please tell me the advantages you have over your black brother who was recently in bondage. Other men owned his field and his house and regulated his pay. His master never refused him enough to live on and never turned him out of house and work, to starve. And you are white men, you the boasted, intelligent American citizens, and vote for these things! Poor Caucasian, little wiser are you hirelings of capital than the chattel slave—he knew he was a slave and that others received all the profit of his labor, but you, you prejudiced biped, you cannot see, or will not see, that a few schemers get all the product of your labor, squander it in riotous living and gaming and leave you as poor as Sambo, and more hopeless. Negroes never committed suicide in their despair, but thousands of you annually do. And you don't know enough to vote against the parties who have done all this to you! And you are Americans.

LINCOLN?

I have just been re-reading the life of Abraham Lincoln, the name revered by the Republican party today, but the principles of whom they detest. I am startled at the similarity of conditions of 1860 and today. The arrogance of the slave-power—the power of a property class to make money out of the labor of others—is duplicated today by the arrogance of the property class that lives in grander style off the labor of others—wage slaves. Those who opposed Lincoln then fought for the privilege of profiting off the labor of chattel slaves—the day is surely coming when the same class of people will fight—or hire ignorance to fight for them—for the privilege of profiting off the wage slaves, who have been more profitable than ever were chattel slaves. Chattel slavery debauched the nation—its congress, courts and presidents. Wage slavery has done more—it has debauched everything. Great corporations buy and sell congress as so many slaves. They have usurped the government. They levy their tax or toll on the people at pleasure. They defy the constitution, courts or any other power. They maintain forts and standing armies (private) and tax the people by adding to the price of goods to pay the expenses. They loot the treasury by a three-card monte bond issue. They rake in millions by rotten armor plate contracts. They debauch every legislature to elect to the United States Senate members of their corporations. They feast and fete while the people are starving. The slave power was never so strongly intrenched because it was in one section only. Wage slave owners are intrenched wherever one man must make a slave of himself to another or starve. As the South was used by Johnson to scatter the navy, possess the arsenals and organize to hold their section, so the money power is behind the building of a navy that is second to none, increases of the armories and war munitions, and are preparing to hold the whole country should the people awake and vote against them. Their actions can have no other interpretations. We need no great navy nor army, unless we are unjust to other nations or our own people. The great standing armies of Europe are to keep the people in subjection to the tyranny of titled robbers, under pretext of being used against a foreign foe. No such excuse is valid here and no excuse is ever given. Millions are annually taxed from our people, already groaning in debt, to military preparations. The rich don't care—they can reduce wages to pay the taxes. Will the millions who hold the power open their eyes to plain facts and cease to vote for their own enslavement? Will another Lincoln rise up to lead the people to the abolition of wage slavery? I think the time will produce the man.

KINGS, potentates and tyrants, under one pretext or another, have ruled the working people of the world from time immemorial. To live a life of sensual pleasure and riotous debauchery they have taken advantage of all the ignorance and superstition of the people, sent among them a set of false religious and political teachers, and thus inculcated the "divine idea" of kings, even while

Third Home of the Appeal and Working Force, 1902-1908.

their hands were red with human blood. As children can be taught to believe any absurd story, so the grown-up children have been taught to believe absurd theories, that enable the kings and their supporters to live off the people. These kings, these wholesale murderers, surrounded themselves with palaces, lands, servants and luxuries, and so do the untitled kings of American millionaires today. There is not a whit difference. The men in the field, shop and mine slave day after day, as did their fathers for thousands of years, to enable an Astor, Rockefeller, Vanderbilt, Cleveland and thousands of lesser likes, to live as no king ever did. The working people today are so many slaves, they dress in clothes their useless rulers would spurn, they live in houses their useless rulers would not stable their horses in, they eat what their useless rulers would not have enter their palaces. The American rulers tax the people without the people's consent. They never ask the consent of the people when they raise the price of the stuff they feed and clothe their slaves with. It is the same old game—the same robbery of the working people.

For the life of me I can't see how a working man, who, while toiling and skimping every day, sees his neighbor always dressed up, always attended by servants, always spending as much as fifty or a hundred working men's wages and never doing any useful work—I say I can't see how the working man can other than regard him as he regards the tyrants who robbed and murdered his ancestors. How a working man can vote the same ticket—well, he who does deserves to be a menial slave. He is fit for no other sphere. He needs a master and will always have one and will serve him like Sambo served his. America is today the home of more potentates than any monarchy. Palaces rise on every hand and the squalid huts of the working people are huddled more thickly like so many pig pens. These brawny working people still listen to and believe all the well-fed, well-housed lawyers and religious(?) teachers tell them. They are led by their prejudice to the polls at every election to support for office the men nominated by those "reputable" citizens who profit by this system at the expense of their ragged fellows. The wives of kings spurned the wives of working people thousands of years ago. Not a monopolist, not a tyrant, not a briber of court, legislature or congress, not a millionaire could maintain his power for a month if the working people could see the glaring fraud and would vote for the public ownership of all monopolies. Every workingman would then have an elegant home, elegant furnishings, elegant clothing, excellent and abundant food, his wife and children could have the advantages that now only the rich who do not work have. Why, O why, working people, will you not vote for a change that will benefit you and those you love so dearly? Why will you remain dupes to these lying politicians just as our forefathers were duped by the lying politicians and tyrants? You think such a condition for you is a dream because those in power tell you so? Your forefathers believed the same lie. Break away from your master's advice, read "Merry Endland," or some other books of that kind, and you will be convinced. It is a fact. It is all yours for your asking it by your ballot. If you vote against it and a majority vote against it, of course it cannot be enacted into law because a majority say by their votes they do not want it. O, laboring people, I beg you, for the sake of your wives and babies and my wife and babies, to read and help us bring about such a glorious adjustment of society. It is simple. All can understand if they desire to. If it is true, you want it; if not true, a little study will prove it. Millions all over the world believe it, they have studied it— do you think they are all senseless dreamers? Read, vote and let us make a new civilization. Let us abolish the poverty and crime caused by private monopoly.

THE INCOMPETENT WORKING CLASS.

I am often told that the working class have not sense enough to operate the government. So far, the working class have not exhibited wit enough to take possession of their government, but they are actually doing all the work of government. There is not a report made by the head of any department of the government that men on salaries do not prepare for their "superiors." The working class — wage-earning class — fill every position of government that requires skill and ability. The heads of these departments from top to bottom are filled with men elected by the working class and who, as a rule, never had any knowledge of the duties of their office. The incompetent get all the glory and the highest salaries. The working class fill the armies—except the officering of it. The working class are able to run the government, but prefer to be hirelings—giving the credit to incompetents.

SAY, my brother workingman, lend me your sun-burned ear for a moment. You are working for some man or corporation? Yes. And they make a profit off your labor? Yes. And they are actually gathering in millions? Yes. You live in the poorest part of town where rents are cheapest? Yes. And you wear the cheapest, coarsest clothing? Yes. And you have coarsest food? Yes. Well, wherein was a black slave in the South any worse off? Did not his master make a profit (but never millions) from his labor; didn't he live in the shanties, dress in coarse clothing and have coarse food? But you have your liberty? Yes, and sorry you are when you have it—you are walking and begging for a master to let you slave for him. Your liberty means starvation, because your masters today own all things you must have or perish. But the slaves were sold apart, father from wife, and children from both. Yes, occasionally, but very seldom. You don't have to leave home and wife to find a master, do you? Your children don't have to leave home, often a thousand miles, to find a master to employ them, do they? Your daughters do not have to leave home to make a living, do they? Whose daughters fill the houses of prostitution because they have had to leave the home roof and mother's loving care? Whose sons, failing to find a master, hunger and are forced into crime and prison, or become drunkards? You are a great deal better off than the slave on old master's plantation, I don't think.

Now, my brother, another word. Do you think the men who grow rich off your labor are going to instruct you how to get out of your present bondage? Did you ever hear of a slave owner telling his slaves how to get away from him? Yes, there is a way to work without being employed for the profit of any man or corporation: Public ownership of the means of production and distribution. In a simpler form—public ownership of all monopolies. Do you know of anybody making a profit off the labor of the letter carriers? Not a bit. Do a little reading on socialism, brother, and you will discover something of more value to you than all the wages ever paid to you in your life. You need new and better ideas, before you will have new and better conditions of life.

It is not often that the printer yells for "copy" at me, but the weather the past week has almost prostrated me. And that, too, under the most favorable conditions. What do the poor fellows suffer out in the broiling sun, heavy with exercise? "Oh, they are used to it," I hear an apologist for the present anarchy reply. Yes, and so were the chattel slaves used to it. But that did not make it right. I notice it is far more pleasant on the shady side of the street watching the slaves in the gas main trenches than getting down there and taking part of the load. This system is all right—so long as enough men can be had to do the dirty, hard work, while us useless fellows take the easy, genteel, better-paid jobs. But what if these white slaves should become wiser than the black slaves? Suppose they should actually begin to compare their pay and labor with the pay and labor of us who take the world easy? Suppose they should actually decline to do the dirty, hard work unless they got the most pay? You would probably call out the militia to shoot them for insurrection, just as the slave owners of forty years ago would have done. But if there is to be any difference in the pay of labor, it should certainly be in favor of the hardest or most essential labor. We could get along without nine-tenths of the merchants, lawyers and bankers, but we could not get along without the people who build our houses, make our clothing or produce our food. The last are essentials without which there could be no civilization. The workers are many and the drones are few, but the drones get the workers to vote the ticket they put up and divide them over some sham fight, and as a result we have nine working men, baking in the hot sun producing wealth and living from hand-to-mouth, and one man who don't do a useful act, getting the cream of what the nine produce. But the nine are used to it, you know, like the slaves, and don't see how a working man is entitled to live comfortably!

My brother, you with calloused hands, who labor late and early whenever ill-fate does not deprive you of place, is it because you do not do your part in the creation of the fabulous wealth of the United States that you are poor? Have you been indulging in palaces and banquets and servants and travel that you now have to struggle for a living? You have always done what those in authority over you directed, eh? And still poor? Why are you poor if you have helped produce the surplus wealth above what has been consumed by society? How comes it that others own the houses, lands, railroads, food, clothing—everything? Have the others been doing so much more work every day and living on so much less than you that they have saved all the billions? Or, are you not in about the same relation to your work and your employers that Sambo and Dinah were on Southern plantations—the more they worked the richer master got? Do you think it was right for the master to take the entire proceeds of the slaves' labor and spend it on himself, leaving them only enough for food and shelter? Of course you don't. The starry banner must float over no slaves. But how much more than these slaves do you get? Are you as certain food will always be for your family? Are you as sure that a house will always be above their heads? Are your employers as interested in your health, sending physicians and nurses in your sickness? Not by a blanked sight, my bamboozled friend. Your condition is worse than a chattel slave, but you do not realize it. All your labor goes to make more millionaires, build more elegant palaces than ever master knew, spread more costly banquets than ever missus presided over, buy more elaborate toilets than ever adorned a Southern beauty, and of late is used to buy titles of reprobate families of Europe. This will be your fate so long as the social structure is based on private ownership of property used in production—so long as you get your political ideas from men on friendly terms with our great people—so long as you depend on anybody for knowledge you should learn for yourself as you did the multiplication table. Read the books on political economy *that your masters do not want you to read.* The truth will make you free—a condition you do not even know of.

TRUTHS IN PARABLES.

I KNEW a company of men owning a very fine estate and on this estate was great wealth in all the things necessary to wealthy owners. These men employed a number of servants at an agreed wage to do the necessary work to maintain the estate and gradually improve it, for the owners were liberal and progressive and desired to leave as a heritage to their heirs an estate even better than their neighbor's. Well, these servants drew their pay, took possession, made all the regulations concerning the estate, increased their pay, squandered the resources of their trust, built themselves fine mansions and mortgaged the farm to pay for them, gave great balls and "Mondays," reduced the owners to beggary and hired them to be servants of the servants. You will say this is all nonsense and twaddle, and such it sounds like. You will say no men with sense enough to own an estate would do any such a thing. Very well. But if you will put the people in this nation as the estate owners which they are, and the various bodies of law makers and judges and officers as servants, for which they were hired, you will see who is foolish and where the twaddle comes in.

ONCE upon a time one hundred men went into business, in which each had one vote in the management. There was much hard work and a few places the duties of which were light—the hours short and the places of work pleasant. When the places were assigned, each filling the one he was best fitted for, the matter of pay came up. It was voted by an "overwhelming majority" that the ninety-five places of hard and dangerous character should work ten hours a day and get $1.00 each, while the easy, pleasant places should work but eight hours a day and get $5.00 a day. Do you not think they were wise to make such rules? That shows how unselfish the majority was to vote on themselves the hard work at low pay and the light work at big pay to the few. Did you ever hear of a country where such things are done? And yet some people insist that the human family is selfish.

A REFLECTION OF SELF.

A man rode a donkey on a very long

and rough journey. Feed and water were scanty and care for his donkeyship was the least thought of the master. Finally the back of the beast became sore and he complained of the load and insisted that the rider should get off and walk. To this the rider objected, but says "I will institute a reform that will ease you; I will increase the tariff and establish civil service." And he nudged back a little off the sore and the donkey, feeling somewhat easier because the pressure had been removed from the sore spot, went on with little complaint. Finally a gall sore was raised on the new point of pressure and the donkey said, "Now I am tired of this and I want you to get off and stay off." But the rider replied, "I cannot do this, but I tell you what I will do; I will institute a new reform that will give you relief; I will revise the tariff." And he nudged forward a little. And thus he cajolled the donkey with promises and deception for the long journey of life, pretending to pity him and feeding him on hopes that tariff, free trade fiat money, gold standard, free silver, imperialism and other nostrums would be just as good as getting off his back.

That donkey is the working mule. He has been carrying his masters through all the ages of the past, eating thistles and having his back worn in sores, first fore, then aft, and yet he listens to the oily tongues of the masters who possess all his labor has created. The donkey is a familiar object everywhere. You can see him wherever you look, his stupid face, his ragged clothes, his lean, lank, hungry eyes peering out from a shabby head covering, his miserable stable that answers him for a home. Have you not seen him? He has the strength to knock off those who ride him, but his mind is hypnotized, and he believes, no matter what country he calls his home, that he is one of the freest mortals and that his country is the grandest on earth. Poor donkey.

SEE this picture: On a broad landscape, with the road bordered here with meadow, there with woodland, we see a team drawing a heavily loaded sled. It is summer and nature smiles in glee. But the driver is urging his team with profanity and the lash to greater speed. It is fruitless. We hail the driver. We explain to him as best we can how he may pass a timber crosswise under the sled and fit a "wheel" on each end, by which means his team may pull a heavier load with more ease and speed. A curl of his lip shows the disdain. "See here," says he, "I have heard of you people before. There are several more crazy men like you around here. My father and grandfather used this sled and it's good enough for me. I am afraid of your new-fangled notions. You may be all right in theory, but it won't work out in practice." And he drives on, muttering something about fool cranks.

Reader, is the picture familiar? Have you ever met any animals like the driver who knows more about the political system we want to bring in than you who have been studying it? Who prefers the poverty, hunger and dirt of his fathers, than the luxuries and elevation of juster methods? Who undertakes to talk learnedly on a subject on which he is as ignorant as a donkey? Who sets up his "experience" of a few years in a narrow round of drudgery against the accumulated wisdom of ages? But be not discouraged. The elevation of man from the ignorance, superstition and brutality of the bygone centuries has been slow, tedious and against his will. He is the typical school boy who does not want to learn.

BE kind, forbearing, but persistent, and we will elevate him in spite of himself.

AND I saw several monkeys with clubs in their hands, and they strutted about the forest which was filled with other monkeys gathering cocoanuts, and they beat these other monkeys when they caught them eating any of the nuts they gathered. And there was one pompous monkey who came and inspected the pile of nuts they gathered, of whom the monkeys with clubs appeared to be in mortal fear, for they crawled up to him like whipped dogs, though either of the club monkeys could have thrashed the life out of him, monkey fashion, and the nut monkeys maintained silence during the pompous monkey's presence, and gathered nuts faster and handled them with greater care. At night the nut gathering monkeys went away and they were given one-tenth of the nuts they had gathered, and a new set of monkeys with clubs relieved the ones on duty. They were to guard the nuts from the nut gathering monkeys. And there came another troop of monkeys and they gathered up the nuts and carried them to the tree of the pompous monkey. And I noticed that the monkeys with clubs took with them about three times as many nuts as the nut gathering monkeys had given them. But what puzzled me most was why the nut gathering monkeys, who outnumbered the ones with clubs ten to one, should be in such mortal fear of them, and why the monkeys with clubs were so abject before the one pompous monkey, who did not even have a club to defend himself. All these things seemed so ridiculous, and I thought that the monkeys had a new game to amuse themselves instead of the one of mimicry. So I went to the tree where the nut gathering monkeys were, and I found them bare and the little ones crying for something to eat and the old ones dividing the scanty nuts among them and not taking enough themselves. Then I hunted the tree of the pompous monkey. It was a glorious tree loaded with nuts, and all about were piles and piles of nuts, and around were many other lesser but pretty trees, in which I noticed the monkeys who carried the clubs, and they also had plenty of nuts, but not great surplus. And I began to think: Here is evidence that man is descended from the monkey, for man does just this way in every land under the sun. He gathers the wealth of the world, it is guarded by foremen, police, militia, army and navy to see that he gets only the smallest share that he can live on, and he garners the results of his toil and genius into the bin of the few idlers and heaps up wealth for them to squander and lavish on their servants and soldiers, and starves amid the plenty he has created, shivers amid the palaces he has erected, and goes ragged amid the beautiful clothing he has fashioned. This is not a dream; it is a literal fact as to man, but a fiction as to the monkeys, for anyone knows that monkeys have too much sense to gather nuts for any other monkey to munch. Yes, we are civilized! Man is a great animal — the apex of wisdom! He shoots his brother workers because they will not take a less share of the nuts they gather for their share! This reverie came to me as I read the accounts of the Brooklyn street car strike and I wondered when civilized man would have the intelligence of the tribes of the trees of the tropics.

WILLIAM MORRIS, the celebrated English philosopher, artist and poet, wrote a fable, which I shall Americanize for your benefit: About Christmas time the poultry of a certain country held a great convention for the good of the race, at which it was resolved that the most important subject to poultry was

"WITH WHAT SAUCE THEY SHOULD BE EATEN." Many prominent members of the meeting aired their various views on the subject. There was a large following that adhered to tariff for protection sauce; others contended that free trade sauce was the thing; others for labor union sauce; others, single tax sauce; others for public ownership of railroad sauce; others for paper money sauce; others for imperial sauce; others for anti-trust sauce. When they had worried over these until the boldest rooster had grown hoarse and the hens had ceased to cackle, a battered old barnyard cock got the floor, and, much to the surprise and disgust of the vast assembly, declared that he did not want to be eaten at all! He was immediately set upon by the poultry working class and turned over to the police, with execrations for being a socialist, anarchist, disturber of the peace and general nuisance. The assembly then ordered that their resolutions be engrossed and sent to the head poulterer. Can you draw the moral?

PRIVATE OWNERSHIP AND THE TRUSTS.

In ye olden time when the king was the law and the state, he often granted some truckling knave, for furnishing him some illicit pleasure, a monopoly of selling all the salt, or fish, or other articles, in this place or that, that the truckling might pay himself out of the hides of the people. That, we are told, was tyranny that no intelligent people would stand, even if it took the last drop of their blood, blood, blood, to wipe out. We do not do such things in these enlightened days, not us! We do not permit one man or set of men to control our oil, or sugar, or meat, or other necessaries! Not a bit of it. We are a free people, and every one is free to do as he likes so long as he infringes not the equal right of every other one! Suppose this nation were to confer the right by law to the Standard Oil Company to sell all the oil in one-half its territory, do you think it would accept? Not much. It absolutely controls more than that at the present time and sees in the future the certainty that it will control all of it in a few years. This is a matter of law as much as the king's fiat. Not a law of commission, but of omission. When the nation refused to go into the oil business it left the field for him who could conquer, and, of course, the conqueror turned up. Oil would be selling at not more than two cents per gallon at every hamlet in the land had it been conducted by the people for the people. The effect is just the same as if the government by law had granted the Standard Oil Company the exclusive right to sell the people oil. The tyranny is just as great. While the people would not have stood the granting of the special privilege by law, they will suffer the evils that would have flown from that method when it is done under a different form. Whenever any people accept the divine right of kings, whether they choose one or not, they may rest assured that someone will fight his way to the top and rule over them, killing perhaps millions in the struggle. It is just so in industry. When the people leave the prize to him who can reach it, someone, sooner or later, will monopolize the necessities and rule over the people with an iron hand. Tyranny has always been industrial—never can be anything else.

It is the products of the industry of the people the master are after. Titles are only the gold lace trimmings to the coat of industrial mail.

THROUGH YOUR MUDDY BRAIN.

Let me illustrate a problem in economics: Suppose the citizens of a community should desire to have waterworks to supply the needs of the people. They would have to pay the cost of such service, whether private enterprise did it or whether they did it publicly.

Suppose, now, that instead of having one large plant sufficiently great to meet that supply, regardless of how owned, they should build ten or twenty or fifty little plants, which combined would give the desired services. Which would be the reasonable way?

You can readily see that if a number of small capitalists owned these small plants that they could not operate them with the same economy as one large plant. The same conditions, of course, would be attached to the plants if owned by the public.

What I want to get you to see is that many little plants would be a very wasteful method, regardless of how owned, to supply the products they want, and that the citizens, somehow and somewhere, would have to pay the necessarily added cost. This proposition is so plain that you will likely laugh at me for trying to get you to see something that everybody can see. But your vision is not so clear when I substitute the word "food" for water. For you insist that the more stores, the more competition you have, the cheaper you get goods, and you refuse to see that all the rents, taxes, heats, lights, interests, advertising, bad debts, delivery wagons, idle time of clerks waiting for customers, are expenses that many stores must put upon you in increased price of goods, just as certainly as you would have to pay these things or forty water corporations, as you now have stores to supply you with practically the same thing; and just as you would be at the mercy of one water company if it were owned by individual interests, so you would be at the mercy of one store if it were owned by a large corporation.

BUT if you owned the waterworks collectively, you would get the lowest possible cost of one plant, as you would get your goods in one store if the public owned that store, just as it now owns the postoffice. There is no more sense, reason or logic in having from a dozen to a thousand stores in a place than there would be in having from a dozen to a thousand postoffices or water plants.

Can't you get that through your noggin?

THE HOW OF IT.

How will socialism be established? By the necessities of the people. This means that the corporations will go on monopolizing, concentrating, lowering wages, increasing prices of goods, throwing so many thousands out of employment by reason of better methods of production and distribution, that the people CANNOT stand the pressure. They will see the oppression from great aggregations of wealth and will in time get desperate. When they take the notion to change things, which they will, they will discover that they need these great organized industries to supply the needs of the people; they will further discover these great industries cannot be divided up into thousands of little ones, because they would then be useless. The machinery of a great factory or a railroad is only useful when all its parts are working together. The property therefore cannot be divided up among the people. If it is left with those in control the oppression will continue. There will be only one thing to do. The corporations will have to be made public property.

AMONG the hundreds of letters that come to me weekly I notice that not a small number believe that what is termed the middle class are the dependence for any reform. I differ with these. There will be and are men of some means who are earnest reformers, but as a class those who have a little property believe they will escape the clutches of the monopolies and that their children will be all right if they can only leave them a little money and an education. The people are not amenable to any logic so long as these ideas control them. They are living in the past and do not see that the industrial conditions have undergone a revolution in the last forty years. There will be no change until this class is wiped out by concentrated capital. This will be virtually completed in the next five to ten years. When they are reduced to the level of the millions of hopeless tenants and vagabonds they will be forced to see the idiocy of their conclusions. Of this class the most stupid is the small retailer. Inside the next two years, this class will begin to see its fate. The new factor of combining one store of each line into a magnificent department store in towns of two thousand and up will rapidly driven them out of business. These stores co-operating will occupy the field and destroy not only the other stores in their own town, but will destroy the stores in smaller towns adjacent. When a chain of these stores are established they will come in the market by millions of dollars at a time and will be stronger than even the great department stores of the big cities. The bankrupted middle class will soon bring a change, but so long as they are the middle class they will oppose any change.

DIFFERENCE IN NAMES.

A reader wants to know the difference between the terms Corporation,

Combine, Trust and Syndicate. As I understand it, a Corporation is a legal entity composed of members to carry on some business. A Combine is where two or more corporations or men make an agreement on what prices they will pay for labor or material and at what price each will sell its productions, while maintaining separate ownership and control their various plants. A Trust is where corporations or individuals put their properties into the hands of trustees to be managed for the benefit of all concerned for some given time or benefit, but the title to the properties are not wholly alienated from the original owners. A Syndicate is a corporation organized for the purpose of buying all the plants from the original owners and operating them for the benefit of the stockholders of the syndicate, who may or may not be the same as the former owners of the various plants absorbed. In effect, all these differ in degrees of the same thing—there being a difference in form but not in the object of the association. In a legal sense, a syndicate is a corporation, while a combine and a trust are not. A syndicate is legal, being simply a gigantic corporation or company, but the courts have decided that trusts and combines are illegal. Syndicate ownership will supersede all other forms of ownership because it offers complete power over production and employment and profits are merely a matter of expediency, at the whim of the board of trustees, who can raise and lower the price of their productions at will.

THE world moves and human progress is not to pay tribute to monopoly or stop and don't you forget it. The people must now master these monsters or be mastered by them. By no use of money shall one man or corporation draw from the producers a part of the product of their toil. We understand well enough that the abolition of chattel slavery was mere child's play to the task before us, but never were men imbued with the holy fire of justice as they are today. When the people will a thing, that thing is done.

CAPITALISM is not wholly bad. While it is crushing the people into direct poverty and crime, it is at the same time teaching the lesson that goods can be made and distributed under the system of largest production with the least amount of labor, and that the greater the plant the more economical. The people would never have consented to public monopoly had the trust not demonstrated its benefits, but they will in the future take over these monopolies into their own hands and operate them for the good of all, instead of for the benefit of a few, as is now being done. In the development of society, capitalism will have played its part for good as well as for evil.

YOU often meet the argument that the great fortunes are distributed and the great firms and corporations break up, and therefore it is foolish to get nervous about the concentration of wealth. This is what the rich people tell their dupes to keep them from thinking. Let us look at it just a minute. A millionaire dies and his sons squander the estate. Who gets it, the working people? Not much. All the houses and lands and factories pass into the hands of richer men. Poor men or small propertied people never get them. What the sons usually squander it on are articles and service that only the rich operators can furnish. A great commercial house fails. Do you find the assets in the hands of the masses, from whom they have been gathered during years gone by? Not a bit of it. They have gone to banks or other great commercial houses, and in either case it means a few wealth holders are richer, *and there is one less of them*. This process is going on rapidly and is going to continue so long as the present system lasts and the time is not far distant when all the property will pass to a few families, as it did in Rome, and we shall have a nation of menials who can only work or eat at the pleasure or whim of a few men, who care not so much for human happiness as they do for their dog. Let me point to you also that our rich people love and long for titles of nobility and are paying millions for them. There is not a drop of patriotic blood for a free country in their criminal, useless bodies. Yes, wealth is concentrating, and when the Belmonts, Morgans, Astors, Vanderbilts, Fields and a few hundred more succeed in getting titles to eighteen billions of the assessed values of American property all the other people will have nothing, for that is all there is of our national wealth. A few thousand of them now own three-fourths of all, hence all the other people can only have the other fourth, which is the whyness of all the poverty and oppression of the masses, and why it is so much more marked now than it was thirty years ago.

IN olden times kings for pay chartered pirates to rob the high seas. It is different now. Kings and governments charter corporations. These go to other lands, rob the people until the people resent it, and then the government that has chartered these pirates on land send a navy to enforce the collection of the alleged damages to the aforesaid land pirates. Such is the wherefore of the navies. After all, they are only pirate ships but used to attack weaker nations, and the robbery is done on the land. Public ownership would change all this.

THE more I study over it, the more I talk to those considered "intelligent," the more I am convinced that no change in the social structure that will give justice to all will be accomplished until the trusts and monopolies shall have possessed themselves of all the property of any value—and not then, unless a socialist party shall have arisen and taught the way. The concentration of all wealth into the hands of a dozen men, and the annihilation of the Roman nation, did not teach the people the way to reconstruct society so as to provide against a recurrence of the condition, and Rome today is either prince or pauper. The people are anxious for a change, oh, yes! But the change they want is one that will prevent the big monopolies from getting so much, but not at all interfere with the small fellows doing business for "profit." They cannot conceive of business being done unless a "profit" is made, and until they are firmly convinced that they can never get a change to make profits, they will not be willing to advocate the public ownership of the means of production and distribution. All the woes of all the people of all nations flow from the one cause: private ownership of what should be publicly owned.

THE debts of any people is the sum of all capital used by labor, the owner of which capital gets, or expects, an income from the mere fact of owning it.

And further, the debt may not be capital at all—may not represent any investment — as, for instance, the so-called capital of watered stocks or bonds. A railroad may have actually consumed $1,000,000 in wages to the men who built it, and that sum is a debt on which the people are required to pay interest as much as if it were a public bond. And if the owners issue five million of bonds and stocks on that road, then the five millions are a debt on which the public must pay. It is none the less a debt because the principal cannot be collected at one time—it is collected in the way of interest but never canceled, or is rather a debt in perpetuity, as is the debt of England to the Rothschilds—a loan made, the principal of which was not to be paid to the loaners. But it was, and is, a debt nevertheless. As finally all interest, rent and profit must be paid in the results of labor, it therefore follows that only those who labor productively can and do pay the annual sum collected for interest, rent and profit, in proof of which we see the title to property, in addition to the annual products, passing into the hands of the income getters.

I DON'T know how it seems to you, but to me it seems that life is one continual struggle and disappointment. From the time we are forced to tackle the struggle for bread it is one desperate fight. The lives of nearly everyone are a round of work, sleep, eat; work, sleep, eat. There is never a chance to enjoy life— and as I see it the object of life is to develop and enjoy it. When the time of dissolution comes and the poor devils look back over the fitful dream, their life has been a dreary waste and all they have been permitted to enjoy has been about as much food, clothes and miserable shelter as a chattel slave. And all this that a system might be maintained under which the voice of greed could develop and expand. The masses of people in this land and all other lands are mere machines creating wealth they are not permitted to enjoy. Like idolators, they have been trained from childhood to believe in the things as they are by those who happen to profit by the condition, and they are not permitted to see that it is wrong and degrading. I can see no progress in a system that debases the many that a few may wallow in luxury. All the ills that affect the human family are a result of the present social system, and can be traced directly to the root: private property for profit. Whenever a mind sees the picture of the golden possibility of the new social order, it ceases to idolize the present chaos.

PAUPERISM INEVITABLE.

Mr. Rockefeller's income is said to be $50,000 a day. I am not blaming him for getting it. If it were not him it would be Mr. Jones or Mr. Brown. The industrial system makes it possible for someone to do this and it might as well be him as anyone else. And the time will come, under the present system, in which one man will get many times that much and the other people will have that much less. There is only a limited amount of wealth created and if one gets much all the others must necessarily get less for what they do. If the increase of national wealth amounts to $2,000,000,000 a year, which it has averaged for the last ten years, and a thousand men get an income of as much as Rockefeller (and they are getting more) it means that the balance must finally become paupers. The social system is out of true, is impracticable and impossible. It is not producing the results which the majority would like to have, and which they expect, from their labor. But it will go on as it is for some years yet, and the rich men of today will be poor in comparison with what men will be in the next ten years, and poverty such as the world has never yet known will be the portion of the masses. Then, and not until then, will they open their eyes to the very plain fact that they have been deceived about the character of private property, and they will make short work of it. When the change comes it can only produce public property—socialism—for there are only two modes of holding property. One is public property, the other private. The mind cannot conceive of any other relationship of man to property. It must be either one or the other. When the uprising comes, whether in legal order or fierce conflict, the property will be made public and inalienable, for the great industries operated for private profit cannot be left in the hands of the present owners, against whom the struggle has been made, for that would only be permitting the same conditions that had oppressed the people. It would be no change at all. Nor can the victors divide the property among themselves, as they did the church property in France at one time. That would be possible in land, but it is not possible with the great industries, which could not be operated except co-operatively. No satisfactory division there would be possible. It could be made public property or left in the same hands that had oppressed. This is the condition that is being hurried along because Mr. Rockefeller is drawing $50,-000 a day and thousands of others less, though still vast sums, in the same time. And the faster they draw and the more they draw, the quicker will come the time when the masses will wake up to the necessity of doing something. They might learn it sooner and bring it in peace and plenty by studying the matter instead of being forced by starvation to see it, but they still prefer to give their confidence into the keeping of the politicians who serve the richest masters, and these politicians are either ignorant or knaves, or both. Hence we have present conditions with one useless member of society drawing $50,000 a day while industrious men and women are forced by necessity to go in hunger, rags and poverty and ignorance. Let the tribe of the Rockefellers increase. Let their incomes increase. Let them reduce labor to the level of the rat-eating Chinese. Let them lord it over the people like the profligate kings and tyrants of old. Let them glut themselves in greed and look with envy on the pittance received by their industrial hirelings. Only by such conditions will the people turn from their idols of gold and private property. All these will hasten the coming of the New Order which will bring on earth peace and to men good will. Let us rejoice that greed is so rapidly consuming itself.

THE trouble with you is that things you believe wrong are right things, and things that you believe right are wrong things. Of course, you don't believe this, and cannot see the hurt that your present belief does. But our ancestors could not see the hurt believing the divine right of kings did them, nor the hurt of worshiping idols in the varied forms. I doubt much, in fact I am sure, most of the people cannot see the harm done our ancestors by their credulity—for if they did they would see at once the same credulity and the same hurt today—changed in name, but the same essence still. The poverty, ignorance and oppression of our ancestors was none the less hurtful because they did not believe it came from supporting a class of idle, vicious people. So today, their posterity is supporting a class of lawless, idle, mischievous, extravagant and criminal people in all the luxury and power of kings, simply because they do not believe their ills come from that source. And many who dimly connect the wealthy and non-producing class with their ills, steadily refuse to believe that the remedy is public ownership instead of private ownership. This belief in the things as they are prevents them from seeing that not riches but the private ownership of riches is what hurts, nor can they see that present conditions are the result of present beliefs. In their defense or belief in private property, they imitate their ancestors' defense and belief in the king's right to rule, to tax, to kill. It is the ability of men to see these things in their true light that the world has termed philosophy. Truth is simple, but it has been surrounded by a thousand lies, so that the working people could not see it, and thus, in following a false belief, become the servants and slaves of the deceivers. This is just as true in the United States as it is among the naked savages of Africa. Every false belief furnishes opportunity for somebody to steal from working people. Now, my dear reader, take your beliefs down, turn them over and see how you came to believe them. If you can do this without prejudice, it is the best way in the world to get wisdom—truth. Belief or faith is no evidence of a fact.

WHAT more can titled monarchs have than those Americans who are crowned with pilfered wealth? What more of liveried servants, cringing menials, flattering courtiers, palaces, balls, drunken orgies and lewd relations? What more of power over life and death, compared with the deadly blacklist for not giving royal obedience in thought to capitalistic master? Wherein differs the menial submission to royal monarch, or employing knave fat with speculative plunder? What more of liberty has a hireling in a republic owned by a few, than a hireling in a monarchy owned by a few? Are not laws in a monarchy made by those and for those who own its wealth, and against those who make its wealth yet have none of it? And are not laws in the United States made by and for those who own its wealth and against those who make its wealth yet have none of it? Titles are incidental, empty baubles; ownership of land and machinery are real—the power behind the throne, the power behind any court and all power everywhere. Where private ownership of land and machinery is allowed, there is monarchy upheld; there is the cunning hand of tyranny; there is the germ of equality that will ripen into despotism and destroy the nation as certainly as thousands of nations have perished, and from this one and no other cause. First poor, then slowly gaining in wealth and power, then concentration of this wealth into the hands of a few, then chaos and destruction. Such has been the history of every nation on earth. Such will be written of the United States by the historian of the next century. Every nation on earth today is rotten at the heart from this same disease—it is universal and the collapse will be universal. The rulers feel the trembling and seek to insure their power by dividing their pilferings —by putting their eggs in several baskets. Thus rich Americans are buying estates and investing in other nations. Kings invest in other nations, so that if an upheaval unhorses them they can fly the realm and live in luxury still on the stolen sweets of Labor's sweat. A taste of bread won from another makes cannibals of men. It is like a man-eating lion—no other satisfies the damnable appetite. The whole mind and soul is poisoned by the taste of unrequited human labor. Look to the near future for the awful sequences.

THE LAND AND TAXATION.

TAXATION WITHOUT REPRESENTATION.

When the oil trust wants money it taxes the people for it. When the king wants money he has to ask the people for it. When the telegraph fellows want money they tax the people for it.

When the sugar trust wants money it raises the price of sugar and the people pay the tax.

When the biscuit trust wants money it taxes the people by a raise in the price of bread and crackers and candy.

When the coal combine wants money it raises the price and the people pay the tax.

When the meat barons want more money they cut the price of cattle and raise the price of meat and the people pay the tax.

When the lead, leather, cotton, wool, wheat, iron or other barons want more money they tax the people by raising prices or lowering wages.

And they do these things without the people having a voice in the matter, notwithstanding that the idea of taxation without representation was shot to death (so the people think) in the Revolutionary War. These taxes are levied on the people for the benefit, in nearly every case, of British nobility who own large, if not controlling, interests in these modern schemes of taxation. How these fellows must chuckle at the squirming of the Great American as he bends his back to the load while his head is filled with bombast of how we licked the British! The British today draw a thousand times as much revenue out of the hides of the Americans as King George wanted them to pay. Taxation without representation, eh? Ye gods, but wouldn't the Americans lick all the kings on earth before they would submit to such tyranny? The public taxes the people pay, while enough to feed the entire nation, is a mere nothing to the private taxes levied on them by these modern barons and paid out of their hides without so much as asking their leave. And under this system of taxation men sink into the lowest depths of poverty and woe, and do not see the covered hand that strikes them down. No king would dare to exercise this power, for he would cause a revolution that would wipe him off his throne, but under the cover of the rights of private property this thing is done openly and the people do not see the cheat. And thus will this nation perish.

Do you believe in taxing men or property? If you say men, then you favor each man paying the same tax, rich or poor—and you know you do not favor that. If property, then why not tax it? You do? Yes, for the state and county purposes, but not national, which is the greatest tax. Let me give you an illustration: The national tax is $500,000,000 a year, or about $40 for each family, which is paid by rich and poor in about the same ratio. If the government tax was raised as is county and state tax, from each according to his property, 31,000 families that hold three-fourths of all the property in the United States would have to pay three-fourths of this five hundred millions a year, or $375,000,000. Do you not see why these families are anxious to have the amount raised by a tariff and internal revenue system? To do so would relieve the masses of that much of the burden, which would have the effect of raising wages. The rich are very anxious to help the poor! And the poor are fighting each other to have more tariff to raise money for the rich contractors. What queer animals are men, anyway; they cannot see a cheat so plain.

BRIDGES were once private property, and toll collected to enrich the owner. The public got tired of that, provided a public fund and made them free—or tried to. But the man who had been collecting toll did not propose to give up his easy way of living without a struggle. So he persuaded the public to build more bridges and borrow his money and pay him interest. Today he sits around and draws his toll from the public treasury, which is cheaper and less troublesome than the old method of stopping every traveler and making him deliver. They found this much better—for themselves—and have applied it to churches, schoolhouses, county, state and municipal improvements. The toll taker is still here, gathering more and more each year—he has only changed his methods. He still lives in the same sumptuous style, surrounded by servants, and the people who keep him up are living in blissful ignorance of the fact that his wealth and their toil and poverty have any relation. He and his friends are still persuading the people that this is the best system on earth and that those who think a better can be operated are dreamers and enemies of society. So long as the people believed they could not live without a king, they killed people who offended the king.

WHO PAYS THE TAXES.

Jones pays the freight—but who the deuce pays Jones? All taxes are paid, and only paid, by the men who produce useful articles. In fact, all expenses of whatever nature or character are paid by the usefully engaged working class, and whenever anything is used to administer to the needs or pleasures of any person not so engaged with mind and muscle that thing is robbed by some device or other from the working class. It does not in the least alter the case if the non-producers are working — even at the most slavish labor — unless the labor is in itself productive. A large per cent of the people of all nations who are working with brain and brawn are as much non-producers and leeches as if they were lolling in idle luxuriousness. All people in armies, in law, in personal service, as servants and lackeys, and in the making of useless ornaments, are non-producers—all are on the shoulders of and supported by unpaid useful labor.

Let us take two sets of men and put them apart—on two islands or in two counties. Put one set to useful labor and they will provide all food, clothing, shelter, instruction and entertainment they can use and have the enjoyment of them. The other set, producing nothing but law, armies, lackeys and useless ornamentation, will starve. Should we find these people enjoying in abundance the things raised by the useful laborers of the adjoining community, when they had produced nothing to exchange for them, we should know they were thieves. But when we mix these people up in the same community we find the useless enjoying in abundance all the useful things and all the useless things, while the useful citizens are allowed to enjoy neither, and look upon this anomaly as right and just! So we have been educated that we may not realize the robbery, like the Mohammedan children are educated to submit to the conditions imposed on their credulity that the masters in church and state may fatten off their labor. When I paid more than a thousand a year in taxes it was first collected of the more or less useful laborers who used the property. They, not I, paid the tax. I was only the agent for its collection—putting most of it in my purse, because of the law which their ignorance sustained. When the tenants failed to pay, I could pay no tax, and if they never could pay no one would want to own any more property than he could use and care for. The man who employs labor non-productively to human needs commits the greatest of all crimes.

THE LAND AND TAXATION.

If one man owned all the land, he could compel all the others to do as he pleased or get off the earth. It would not be to his interest to drive the people off, for then the earth would not bring him anything unless he would labor on it, and that is what he don't want. What is true of one owner is true of many. All who do not own must and do pay to those who do own the privilege of living on the earth. It does not impair the fact that one or a small minority could not enforce eviction off the earth—the majority can hedge them with rules that will prevent that, but in doing so they also deny the right to complete ownership and, so far as morals are concerned, might as well deny the right to own land at all. In fact, no one does own land and can draw no rent from it except the law ostensibly made by the majority permits it.

The individual hoe-maker has disappeared.

The individual wagon-maker has disappeared.

The individual watch-maker has disappeared.

In fact, individualism in production has almost entirely disappeared, the workers being only parts of machines and having nothing to do with the products or their price when they have done their work. There is only one great field of production which has not yet been conquered by the capitalist with the power of capital and great machinery too expensive for the small fellows—that one thing is the farming of the nation. But capital and great machinery are going into the field of agriculture and will soon do up the small farmer just as the small producers in other fields have been done up and forced into wage slavery. Wheat is being raised by capitalistic methods at a cost of wages of $3\frac{1}{2}$ cents a bushel in the sack, corn at 10 cents and other farm products at like low cost. When enough capital is invested in such farming to produce the needed national supply the small farmer will follow his deceased fellow-worker in the small shops and will fall in with the lock-step of the slaves of the agricultural lords of creation who will sit in their fine offices and direct the working operation of the farms as they now do their factories. Men no longer need to know a business to operate it successfully. J. Pierpont Morgan is not a railroad man, does not know anything about the technical terms and duties of the employes, but he owns tens of thousands of miles of railroad, to say nothing of the coal and iron mines and other industries. Capital can hire the slavish brains that will properly conduct any industry and make it millions. In ten years the farming of this country will be done by capitalists who do not know anything about farming, and they will knock the hay seeds off the fellow whom they now make fun of as being too green to burn. Note the picture of farmers that appear in the daily and illustrated press owned by the capitalists. Most of the men on the land today are tenants of small farmers or else hired hands. Tomorrow they will be the hirelings of the great farmer who owns and operates millions of acres of land. And where is your individuality then?

There are a great mass of people so thoughtless that they believe it is well for a community or nation when its real estate sells at a high figure. But just the reverse is true. The higher it is the more your children will have to give of their labor for the privilege of having a spot to live on. Do you think the high price of New York dirt is good for those who have to pay proportionately high for the use of it? Every rise in real estate means that the many of the future will have to pay to the few owners of the future more and more of their labor for the privilege of living on the earth. The lower priced the land and the higher priced the labor the better for the masses of mankind.

WHY don't they do it at once and settle the agony? Do what? Why, confiscate the man's property. Why drag him up to court house term after term, forcing him to neglect his work, worrying the life out of him and his family, paying all he can make to lawyer, sheriff and court officers and then finally taking all he has? Would it not be more humane to take it outright? Is it any less robbery because it takes it by degrees? So many cases like this I have known and the poor victims never once dream that the whole judicial system and the money, contract and land system is a cunningly devised plan for a few of the most utterly worthless of men to eat the fruits of other men's labor. But you don't believe that? Of course you don't. I know well enough you don't, else the thing would not have so long flourished. But the fruits of the system is proof enough. Even when kings oppressed the people, took their property, took their sons and trained them for murder and their wives and daughters for the pleasure of titled roues—I say, even to this day, a large majority of the human race believe the divine right of kings. My statement regarding the courts is true just the same whether you believe it or not. If justice reigned, arbitration would settle all disputes in an hour or two at no cost or delay. But what would the lawyers and such others do then?

IT is more profitable to own the land and make people pay you to live on it than to own the people, body and soul. The land should belong—and does in equity—to all the people and the public should be the landlord, receiving all the rents for the use of it, and this money should be spent for the benefit of all those who pay it by erecting schools, libraries, public buildings and constructing roads, pavements, parks, telegraphs, telephones and railroads. Then would the people begin to enjoy freedom that has been withheld from them ever since schemers induced them to believe that land should be private property. Private property in land is indefensible and has been condemned by all humanitarians and philosophers in all ages.

YOU cannot legislate wealth into existence but you can and do legislate who shall own it when it is brought into existence. And as a rule the title to the property produced by labor is handed over to those who in no wise aid in producing it. A law that allows a king to own certain lands or that gives him an income from certain districts as certainly robs the people who live on that land or in that district as anything can be. It matters not whether his kind buys the land or is given the land. It is of no value to him, produces no income, unless human labor and intelligence is applied to it. It is the law, or the power behind the law, that compels these people to deliver to him a part of what their labor applied to the earth has produced—rank robbery. And it does not matter whether the man is a king or a private citizen, either. The robbery is just as flagrant in one case as the other. If the purchase of the land is recognized by law the robbery will follow just the same. It is a getting of something for nothing. Robbery of the workers will continue so long as any other title but use and occupancy is recognized.

SOCIALISM AND COMPETITION.

There are those who with words deny the law of co-operation is more beneficent than competition regarding wealth production, yet if they desire to do anything at once call in the help of their fellows. There is a field for competition but it is not in the field of property accumulation. It is in the mental field of desiring to do most to help the world to higher planes of living. Competition in good works—not in greed. I do not believe the theory of competition in the industrial field is good. If we will admit that any theory of single or double tax, and theory of hard or soft money, any theory of direct or indirect tax, will enable people to have a home, and an income, I shall then ask you what kind of a home and how much of an income. This is the gist of the controversy. Under which theory will they derive the most and best food, clothing and shelter, instruction and entertainment? Experience and observation has demonstrated nothing clearer than that the greater number of people harmoniously associated the greater the product for a given day's toil. We have passed the stage of farming and manufacturing on a small scale as being wasteful and nonproductive. Good homes cannot be created by small or individual effort. The small farmer, if you give him free land, untaxed, cannot make his labor as productive as if he had the aid of machinery and science, too expensive for isolated application. The same is true with factory and shop. No man can own all the implements necessary to production, and if he cannot he is to some extent at the mercy of those who control his tools. Even if he could, he could not gain that skill in their use that a minute subdivision of labor can achieve. The great factories and farms and stores are displacing the smaller ones under the inexorable operation of the law of economies. I would not deny to people the right of isolated farming. That is their natural right. I would say to them: "By your isolated effort, lack of diversified knowledge, machinery and skill, you produce in a year only one-fourth as much as we who nationally co-operate. Come and be one of us and you can lay down your many burdens and receive four times as much for it. We have the combined capital of millions of people. Each of us has one line of work—no bother or trouble with others. Each of us doing our mite of work, production is completed, and each has all he wants of all the labor of all." Such an argument would have more power than a standing army of force. I would see all farmers so organized, living in the most beautiful towns of ten and twenty thousand that science and skill can build, where they may enjoy the benefits of the highest sanitary condition, heat, light, power, theatres, opera, library, museums, art galleries, parks, drives and all the elevating influences their highest ideals could demand. They could be transported to and from their field of labor on rapid transits at far less expense than the maintenance of the very miserable roads they now wade through.

Factory operatives would also live as beautifully.

All this is more scientific, more practical and more desirable than the present anarchy or lack of head and heart.

Every mind that comprehends this picture longs for it. It will produce more happiness than any amount of individual wealth, with its cares and crosses under the present conditions.

You see my idea is not one of force, but one of love—voluntary co-operation in its final stages.

This is a higher ideal than any tax theory.

INCENTIVE.

UNDER a system in which all could have plenty they tell me there would be no incentive to work. A tenant who gets all the crop would have no incentive—he must give some rent—half he raises for an incentive! Or the man working for a dollar would have no incentive if he got $10.50! People who live in shanties would have no incentive to live if they were furnished good houses with all the conveniences of science! There would be no incentive to board a railroad train at $\frac{1}{4}$ to $\frac{1}{2}$-cent a mile instead of paying the railroad kings 3 cents more. It's too bad about the incentive business.

MAKE it possible for men to get wealth by doing wrong and you will gather a harvest of crime. When men can get wealth of others by adulterating food, or medicines, or clothing, they will do it. But please tell me in what manner could a man profit by dishonesty when he was a producer of wealth as are now the workmen, the title to all wealth being in all the people, and all workers being paid for their time and no extra for adulterating or cheapening an article? The workers today get nothing more for producing shoddy, or dough coffee beans—it's the proprietors who profit. Now make the public the proprietor and it will have no interest in swindling its members. Then all will have plenty for all, the idle rich and idle poor will be given work and will produce the good things of life under a rational system. "If they will not work, neither shall they eat."

You say there would be no incentive to progress if every man had a good home, good clothing, good food and plenty of leisure? Is that why the incentive of the rich is crushed out? Well, if it does, let the people have a whack at the good things just once to see how it goes.

Make it unprofitable for a man to do wrong and he will not do wrong. Take away the profit to individuals in running railroads by having the nation own them and you will not have railroad corporations corrupting senators, congressmen, legislators, judges and other public functionaries. Public men today have a premium set upon wrongdoing, and they reap great profits from their dishonesty and corruption; and they always will do wrong under this incentive so long as human nature is as it is. But this same human nature will not pay out its money if it cannot profit by it. The cause of incentive is private profit. Take away the incentive or cause by having the railroads operated only for the benefit of the people, as is the postal system, and you effectually remove the incentive to corruption and extortion from this source. That this is fair and logical I think none will deny. And it is just as applicable to the telegraph, the street cars, the gas, the water works, the telephone, the coal, the oil, the sugar trust and all other monopolies. If you do not like to be robbed, why do you not support measures that when enacted will make robbery, bribery and extortion unprofitable? If you are men endowed with reason why do you not use your reason? What is reason for, if not to be exercised? Don't blame the monopolists—they are only doing what your votes have made it profitable for them to do. The robbed are many. The robbers are few. When the many vote in a practicable system instead of the present impracticable one the robbery will cease and the people will be prosperous and happy.

People tell me, that is, some people do, that the substitution of public property where now is private property, in business, would destroy the incentive in men that pushes them on today. Granted. But it may prove, on investigation, that that is the very thing to be desired instead of deplored. It may prove to be another idol of ignorance and prejudice,—the people once thought they would relapse into barbarism if they had no king to guide and protect them.

MORAL AND RELIGIOUS QUESTIONS.

ARE YOU A CHRISTIAN?

It is all very nice to talk about solving the unrest and misery of today by leading "Christian lives," applying the "golden rule," etc., but how is a man to love his neighbor for the few crumbs from Dives' table or starve? If the Christian theory is to be a solvent one it must be applied as a whole, and that is what these people refuse to see. As well try to apply mathematics and ignore the existence and value of one of the digits as to try to live a Christian life and ignore the basis of that religion—a community of property. Without a community of property there can be no brotherhood. There could have existed no harmony among the disciples and the early Christians had the laws of competition been recognized. To become a Christian it was first necessary to turn over all property to the common fund or store. No nation has any moral right to claim it is Christian that by law recognizes the private ownership of property. Private wealth is anti-Christian. Men and women who hold to the theory of private property are either ignorant of what Christianity is or else are hypocrites. Socialism goes very far toward the Christian ideal. It would not recognize by law any private title to land or machinery used in production for sale, but these should be operated co-operatively and governed democratically by the workers. By this method there is no competition—strife —between the members of society. The success of one does not mean the loss of others, but the success of each is beneficial to all. Under such a system the Christ principle could be developed; under the present system it can never be, though you put a church on each corner of every square in the land. Tropical fruits will not live in a frigid zone, nor can the golden rule be applied where people recognize the devil-contrived theory of private property and production for profit instead of use.

THE amount paid out for charity in this country every year would furnish the necessary land and machinery for all these recipients to create their own living ever after, while as now operated they have to be provided the next year at the same expense. All this is pure waste and degrading on the recipients. But such is the wisdom that rules the world. That such a sensible system has not been adopted is not because it is not known, but to the fact that the product of such labor would come into competition with one or more branches of production now occupied by capitalists, and they would rather the people would rot than have their business interfered with. It is all right to use these poor people if it adds to capitalists' profit, but the people are not to be allowed to do anything and get all the results of their labor.

PLEASE BE CHRISTIAN.

There are thousands of people out of the churches, and who will have nothing to do with them, who would gladly support them if the ministers would preach the "doctrine and fellowship of the disciples," as laid down in Acts. They beg the preachers to preach Christ's doctrine. There is nothing in creeds and form that appeals to the people who are intelligent. They want something to make the world better to live in. Heaven is all right, but people who are not willing to make such social arrangement here that men may be brothers are hardly the kind to improve Heaven by educating for that condition. Talk to any group of men and you will find that most of them are disgusted with the fawning of ministers to the pews that pay the largest dues, who can overlook the means by which money is gotten, if a criticism of the social arrangement would offend. What the world needs is teaching that will instruct the people how to arrange the affairs of THIS world so that men CAN be brothers. They cannot compete for wealth and feel brotherly. That is what Christ and the disciples taught, and the "common people heard them gladly," and they will heed the same doctrine as gladly today. It is not stated that the wealthy heard the doctrine gladly, nor will they today, but anyone professing to be a follower of the Christ should not ignore the doctrine for that reason. There are millions today who will support teachers who will talk about the affairs of this world, how the production and distribution of God's gifts shall be justly done, that all will have mutual brotherly interest. They are begging the ministers to be Christian. A few ministers are being converted to the Christ doctrine, and they are having the greatest congregations—and of those who otherwise would not enter a church.

"THAT which is holy in Heaven is holy on earth." Do the usurers and monopolists expect to find their occupations going in Heaven? Do they expect to be favored by conditions that will compel the great mass of angels to spend their eternity of time in a ceaseless round of drudgery that they may have more than the average amount of bliss in the New Jerusalem? If it be wrong to think of such things in Heaven, it is wrong to have them on earth. "On earth as it is in Heaven."

WHY are you not as wise as Plato or Aristotle or some of the sages of two thousand years ago? The average man has doubtless read more than they did, but not the same kind of reading. If you would read a few books on the social problem you would soon discover why their names are immortal, and why yours is not. If what they teach were not against the interest of kings, monopolists and the like to have you know certain things, these subjects would be taught in the schools. But because the ruling classes control the schools they are careful to have the books teach such things as they profit by the people believing. If men were wise, if they were not early prejudiced against certain books and sciences there would not be a ragged, hungry person in the land. Knowledge would make them free, but when a few only know and the many don't, the many by their votes uphold the system that produces all the ills of life. Jesus Christ was one of the wise. He was killed by the rulers to prevent His teaching the masses how to live on earth, for if the common people "who heard Him gladly" had been allowed to absorb His teaching they would soon have dethroned tyranny in all its forms and lived in a brotherhood—what reformers now term the co-operative commonwealth.

A NEW religion is being created and is permeating the whole of society. It is not announcing itself with the noise of loud exhortation, but is coming quietly in response to the longing in the human mind for a truer, nobler relationship of man. It is the religion of the Brotherhood of Man and the Fatherhood of God or unity of all nature. As has ever been the case, it is opposed by the established churches, who can never see any good in anything that does not pay tithing to them. For several years I have been watching the slowly crystallizing sentiment creating this new social force and while it builds no churches it is already a power in this and other lands. With the New Social Order of Love and Harmony will come the New Religion. Religions change, just as do civilizations.

MAN has never attained happiness nor ease. In his flounderings about for it he has created conditions in which he cannot harmonize himself. He sometimes assumes that he has been made wrong and cannot achieve harmony or Heaven on earth. If he would reason that he cannot change his nature but can change his surroundings he would be getting near the truth. If harmony prevailed, man would be happy, for unhappiness is simply lack of harmony. Man has been trying to harmonize himself with private property and has never yet succeeded in a single instance and never will, because it makes conditions antagonistic to his nature. Neither the rich nor the poor are happy or at ease. Ease with competition or strife is not possible, because they are opposite. Man is all right, but he has made environments for himself that make his life miserable. This can be remedied by replacing competition with co-operation.

ADDRESSING a Bible class in New York recently Andrew Carnegie said: "It will indeed be a sad day when poverty is no longer with us. Where will your inventor, your artist, your philanthropist, your reformer, in fact anybody of note, come from then? They all come from the ranks of the poor. It is bad policy to aid the submerged man." If there was no poverty there would be no oppression, no millionaires, no kings, no social leeches. The rich want poverty. They want people to be dependent that they may have such service as they desire without having to return like service to their fellow men. If poverty creates inventors, artists, philanthropists and reformers, then the accumulation of riches is a bad thing, because these desirable elements of society are not generated in the families of the rich. That is Mr. Carnegie's argument. There is no question but that individual wealth is destructive to moral development and stifles genius, but intense poverty does the same thing. Neither great riches nor poverty is desirable, are not good for the human family, and a time is coming to men now living when these monstrosities in the social organism will be impossible. With the abolition of private property the opportunity for development will be equal to all and not to those skilled in the cunning of accumulation only. When the working people of the world realize the force of this statement that the rich people desire poverty, then the greatest work in abolishing poverty will have been accomplished. We want the nation wealthy, not the individual.

WOMEN in politics, yes, and the sooner the better. Represented by men, there is no sympathy in politics. It is cold, cruel, relentless scheming. Woman by nature is sympathetic and loving. If there is a case of destitution, not men but women minister to its needs. It is they who nurse and care for the sick out of pure goodness of heart—not men. It is they who never tire of planning little pleasures for others. When they enter politics it will not take long for their intuition to locate the root of the social diseases. Their sympathies can be more readily appealed to than the men's. Men have never studied politics and today, with all their years of exercising suffrage, are as ignorant as the women on matters of state—yes, even more ignorant. The women are ready students. In their home life, even with all the cares of domestic duties, they are freer to read and think than the man who puts in ten or twelve hours' hard labor. And the wives and daughters of the well-to-do are not scheming all day in the store or counting house. I know they spend their time now on dress and balls and parties and weddings, and many will continue to fritter away their lives thus, but the many with the new mantle of political responsibility suddenly thrown on them will begin to investigate. They read books; men read papers. Philosophy is taught in books. There are thousands of women on the lecture platform and every one is advocating something for the betterment of the race. This cannot be said of men. Disfranchised as they are, women have written some of the most powerful books in favor of political reform. Their ideas are higher and their ballots will not long support this system. They have not the same prejudice for it that men have—they will listen and consider. The men won't, especially if they have enough to eat and wear.

THE WISE MAN.

The wise men of the east—press and pulpit—are discussing whether the death penalty should be inflicted for arson, as it is becoming so common. Three hundred years ago the death penalty was inflicted in England for stealing—yet men stole just the same. The wise men of that time, on a notable occasion, consulted as to what should be done to prevent the alarming increase of larceny. They could think of no greater punishment than death and the churches' malediction of an eternity of death hereafter. Although hundreds of thieves' bodies were continually hanging from gibbits, men continued to steal. About that time the lord chancellor of

England in a work told these wise men that if they would let the people employ themselves on the land and not take from them so much rent and profits instead of turning them out and denying them work, that the men would not need to steal; that hunger drove them to it; that no man-made law would prevent men starving or doing other crime if that law violated nature's law. So with these increasing cases of arson. So long as men are compelled by law and custom to have money, and the rapid monopolization of capital is denying them money as a legitimate result of labor, men will kill, burn and rob. If they desire to have crime cease they must make crime unprofitable. If houses and stocks of goods were the whole people's and all lost and none could gain by its burning, where is the fool who thinks anybody would burn houses? Or who would murder to become heir to property if they could not heir any? Or who would steal if they could make a living by honest and respectable work, which everyone could have? With no deeds, bonds, stocks, mortgages or current money, what could men steal that they could get away with? "Lead us not into temptation but deliver us from evil," is very old, but wise people have not yet learned its meaning. Our barbaric system denies men the right to labor, and places wealth before them if they will steal, burn, kill, embezzle or forge, and starvation or want if they remain honest, and then people wonder at the number of crimes! There would be mighty few fires if there were no tempting insurance policies. Still less if all the houses and unbought goods were the property of the nation as they should be.

CAUSE AND EFFECT.

While population has only doubled since 1860, the consumption of tobacco has increased five fold, and, while I have not the statistics at hand, suppose the consumption of liquors has increased as much. The presence of tobacco and liquors is not the cause of the increased use of them. The lack of healthful modes and recreation, the excitement of undue successes and the despair of failures are the prime causes of the use of stimulants. We are often told that we should not judge other people by our own half-bushel, but I know of no other measure but my own consciousness. I well remember the days when I made (legally robbed from society) thousands of dollars. The effect on my nerves was intense and for the first time I felt a craving for liquor and called the boys up to take 25-cent drinks. In times of great depression I have felt the same desire. Great despair or success alike destroy the equilibrium of life and cause dissatisfaction in some way with most people. A state of society that would reward industry, however humble, with its rightful wealth and surround people with elevating pleasures, would not find any increased use of tobacco, liquors and drugs. The use of these things is only an effect of some deeper cause, and the increasing consumption of them shows that cause is working with increased power. That cause is inherent in the system of private property which affords the means of exploitation, giving to some unearned riches and denying to others the rightful results of toil. Nature's laws are inexorable and are not to be set aside by legislative enactment. It is in accordance with natural law that men grow more drunken, more debauched and more brutal under a system that gives the wealth they create to a few cunning men and makes their honest efforts non-productive to themselves, such as the system we live under. If the people want a race of upright men and women, of physically and mentally developed human beings, they must environ them by a social contact entirely different from the present. The present system produces present conditions, and another system will produce other conditions. So long as men suffer excitement or despair so long will they demand stimulants and so long as men can make a profit off that demand men will cater to it, law or no law. Remove private property, thus doing away with speculation and profit, and after one or two generations there will be no artificial stimulants used. Do this not and the present conditions will intensify as wealth concentrates, and drunkenness, arson, murder, suicide, embezzlement, robbery, and all other crimes will go on increasing. No reform is worth the candle that does not change the whole social system.

Present Quarters and Working Force of the Appeal.

MISCELLANEOUS SUBJECTS.

You say I am radical. Well, what of it? Are you afraid of a word? A radical may be right or wrong. Are you not as much a radical in your efforts to maintain the present millionaire-pauper system as I am to change it for better conditions? Never mind about radicalism. If the reformers are wrong, show wherein. A man cannot be too radical in advocating the right. Then the question is, are we right or wrong? Would a system that abolishes poverty and crime be more desirable than the present? Would it be right? Would it not be right if every man or woman who desires to labor that they might create wealth equal to what they consume were given the opportunity and on whom no non-producers should lay tribute? And if so, to what extent? Where is the exact limit that divides right from wrong? If a man produces a bushel of potatoes, why is he not entitled to all the consumers pay for them, with the least expense that they can be delivered to the consumer under the most economic conditions? To assume that one set of men have a right to profit off of others is to assume the right of a slave owner to profit off his slaves. When men are used by others for profit, whether under the name of rent, interest or what not, they are to the profit receiver just the same as the slaves were to the master. The masses have been taught these things are right, just as their forefathers were taught in the divine right of kings, but their believing it does not make it right. The masses have never studied these problems, and they do not know the wrongs injure them, and if they did they do not know that a system can be created that will bring about a remedy. Jesus taught the system and He lived that system—not in reference to a world to come, but in this material world. Pure souls cannot exist in wretched poverty-eaten bodies, and before purity can be enthroned and intelligence developed to receive the teachings of the Saviour, the conditions here must be changed so humanity will live pure. This can never be done under a system of competition—of rent, interest and profit.

MANY years ago, when our forefathers, down-trodden and oppressed by the tyranny of kings, turned their backs upon the scenes of their childhood and their faces toward the new world of liberty in the west, it was with hearts filled with rosy hopes of peace and plenty. Nor were they disappointed. The hardships of pioneer life were more than compensated by receiving the full result of their labor, and happy homes sprung up as if by magic and each newcomer was gladly welcomed as a valuable addition to the social circle. But with the seed of liberty they brought the cockle of usury and usurpation. How different the scene today. The newcomer is spurned and if he succeeds in landing a disappointment awaits him. He finds a land of hunger and rags, men competing with each other for the sake of a bare living, great lords and syndicates usurping the rights and opportunities of the people and dictating with the prerogatives of kings who may and who may not make a living. They find the once glorious haven of the oppressed transformed into a condition of monarchy not unlike that of Europe. The giant of freedom has been shorn of his strength and manhood. The liberties handed down by the founders of our country have been turned over to the banks, monopolists, trusts and combines and are lost to the people. America is no longer the home of the free.

A LEAD ARGUMENT.

I have a friend who once upon a time put in $500 with a few other friends into a hole in the ground which they had reason to believe contained lead. As a result, he and his friends have been drawing $500 a month each for some time, and with prospects of drawing it in the future. It is not drawn under the pretense of their digging lead, or in any wise assisting in its production, but simply because they put in the "capital." Labor takes the lead out of the ground and when the lead is sold part of it goes to the producers and the greater part of it to these people who bought the land. The price of lead is increased to the extent of what is paid the speculators. The public uses the lead, and the public has plenty of capital, as it has plenty of soldiers when it needs them. Do you not think the public, not one in a thousand of whom has any interest in lead mines, is very foolish to pay 100 per cent a month for a little money invested in producing lead for them? Under socialism lead would be mined by the public ior the public, and the price of lead would be the amount of wages paid real workers for mining and smelting it. But perhaps you prefer to pay four or five times as much?

Do you believe that the present system of doing business and holding property will endure forever? Do you really, sincerely think that in the long time to come that great corporations will own and control all the industries as they do today? If you do, you must be something of a pessimist yourself to look to such a gloomy future as that will make. But if you do not, what kind of a change do you think will come? Who will own the industries? How will they be operated? How will all the people be employed when machinery does not work? Are the masses to be servants of the rich as they were in feudal times? And what will become of such as the masters, for any reason, do not want? If private ownership of great industries is today crushing out the small factories and business men, what will it do when they are all crushed out? If these great corporations raise prices today, thus indirectly forcing the people to serve them, will they not continue to do it? And to what extent? And what will become of the people in this raising process? But perhaps you are not interested in these obtuse questions, and had better not answer.

Suppose a ship's crew were cast upon an inhabited land from which there was no leaving, would that fact justify their murder or enslavement by the residents?

Suppose there was an abundance of unused lands, forests and mines; would the inhabitants be justified in refusing it to the comers; would that not be murder? Or suppose that access was granted on condition that the comers work every other day for the residents, would that not be slavery?

Have or have not all men a right to live on the earth? If not, where should they live?

The greater portion of the children born have no recognized right to live on the earth, except as they buy the privilege from the few who have a recognized right. These children did not invite themselves here, nor have the children of one part of the people a right to exact tribute from other children for the privilege of living or working on the earth. There is land enough for all. And some day, not long hence, there will be a just conception of right, and those who desire to use land may have it and those who will not use it shall not keep others from using and retaining the whole of what they produce.

SAID a gentleman who was commander in the Confederate army: During several days' hard fighting there were intervals of cessation when the troops on both sides were tired of killing each other. In one of these the opposing forces were Irish regiments, only a few yards apart, both intrenched. These soldiers were of the same nation, and of the same church largely, and here they were trying to kill each other, and in these moments of intermission were on the breastworks cursing each other for fighting for the Union or the other side. Neither of them had any knowledge of the causes that led up to the war, neither had but little interest in the results, and neither had any excuse for being there except they had followed the suggestions of ambitious or excited men. The gentleman said that at the time it struck him as rather ridiculous that the men under him should fight, as their interests, if any they had, were against human slavery, as they never had any slaves. So it has always been. The great common people have fought each other, at the command of self-appointed leaders, about things they never took time to learn anything about. They killed each other because kings quarreled. They voted against each other because scoundrels want the spoils of government. They never vote for themselves, don't know enough to, and those who profit by their ignorance prevent them from learning. And how wise do they think themselves!

Do you elect statesmen to make laws for you? Or do you elect men who have never studied the science of society? Do you elect men who want office for the salary, the honor, or the good they may do their fellows? Do you elect men who are mere machines, who follow out the lines and rules laid down by those who benefit by things as they are? Do you know what changes, if made, would benefit the people and bring peace and plenty? If you do not, how do you know what kind of a man to vote for? Can you then judge a physician without having any knowledge of the science yourself? Can you then judge a law maker without knowing what ought to be? If you judge by results, and most of the patients of the physician die, would you call him a competent physician? Judging by results while most of the people are in poverty, hunger and dirt, would you call the law makers competent? If liberty is to be maintained in the United States it will be necessary that the voters study the great questions of government—finance, land and labor—or else they will be the victims of designing men who profit off their credulity. The ordinary politician does not read any works that promise any solution for existing difficulties. Suppose you read some of these works and see if you are not convinced that this is a fact.

ONE supreme judge changed his vote from a few weeks ago and the income tax is unconstitutional. Now if Judge

Shiras had voted as he did last month it would have been constitutional. Don't it look like one man changing his opinion changes the constitution? Isn't that actually what has happened? And yet the wording of the constitution has not been changed in a letter! Strange things do happen. Here we are tied by a few words on a piece of parchment, and unless forty or fifty million of people demand it by a tedious process, no change can be made. Yet one man changing his views changes that instrument! The court decided the income tax law, years ago, as constitutional, and now the court decides it is not constitutional! So far as the people are concerned, the constitution has been changed to mean just the reverse of what it meant years ago without their consent. It is a queer state of affairs when the vote of one man can reverse the meaning of a great fundamental law. I am not criticising the verdict nor its legality or sincerity, but am trying to show you the absoluteness and one-man power our judicial machinery is. The majority of people want a law, as expressed by their representatives, and enact that law. It lays in the power of one man to decide they shall not have that law. And these people labor under the delusion they are self-governing people. They elect one set of men to make laws (the legislative), another set to enforce those laws (the executive), and another set to say what the law meant (the judicial). A crude, unwieldy, incomprehensible system.

UNDER direct legislation the people would vote on the laws, and those receiving a majority would be adopted as fundamental (or constitutional) laws. If a court were to decide the laws meant differently from what was intended, a new law correcting it or abolishing the court would at once be instituted by a demand, and submitted to the people. We live in a one-man or monarchy form of government.

EVERY instance of discontent proves the present system impractical.

Every quarrel among neighbors proves the present system impractical.

Every law suit proves the present system impractical.

Every crime proves the present system impractical.

Every court proves the present system impractical.

Every policeman or soldier proves the present system impractical.

Every prison is evidence that the present system is impractical.

Every debt is evidence that the present system is impractical.

None of these things would appear in the social contact if the environment were in harmony with human nature. But human nature revolts against its unnatural restrictions and the frictions quoted result as a natural consequence. Socialism alone will reproduce harmony and love among the members of society, because it is based on the nature of mankind.

It is un-American for you to permit a few well-fed do-nothings to dictate what you shall pay to ride on a railroad.

It is un-American for you to permit a few well-fed do-nothings to dictate what you shall pay to send a telegraph message.

It is un-American for you to permit a few well-fed do-nothings to dictate what you shall pay for coal.

It is un-American for you to permit

a few well-fed do-nothings to dictate what you shall pay for oil.

It is un-American for you to permit a few well-fed do-nothings to dictate what you shall pay for flour.

It is un-American for you to permit a few well-fed do-nothings to dictate what you shall pay for rent.

It is un-American for you to permit a few well-fed do-nothings to dictate what you shall pay for water.

It is un-American for you to permit a few well-fed do-nothings to dictate what you shall pay for gas.

It is un-American for you to permit a few well-fed do-nothings to dictate what you shall pay for electricity.

It is un-American for you to permit a few well-fed do-nothings to dictate what you shall pay for street car fare.

It is un-American for you to permit a few well-fed do-nothings to dictate what you shall pay for any other thing.

OUR forefathers rebelled — actually armed themselves and fought good King George III—because he wanted to tax them six cents a pound on tea without giving them representation. King George was a fool. He ought to have given them a "representative" and then bribed him as is done today. It would have been cheaper and shown better kingcraft. The American people tingle all over with independence and defiance to tyranny and taxation without representation, they do. The Standard Oil Company don't tax them without representation! The railroads don't tax them without representation! The coal combines don't tax them without representation! The sugar trust don't tax them without representation! Four hundred and sixty other trusts don't tax them without representation!! Oh, no! Of course not. The Americans wouldn't begin to stand any such business.

It is amusing to read the proceedings and orations of the meeting of Irish-Americans in convention at Chicago about freeing Ireland from British rule and appealing to all Irishmen everywhere to arm. Just as though a successful rebellion of Ireland against Britain would make Irishmen free! Americans did that thing 120 years ago, but I am quite sure Americans have been oppressed as much or more since, than they were by King George III. It takes something more than successful battles to make a truly free people. It takes ideas of a higher order than the masses of Ireland or America have. If Irishmen would send to parliament a solid delegation demanding free land, free money, free machinery, and ask the co-operation of Scotch and English working people who are just as badly oppressed, Ireland would soon be free. But to depose the English parliament and put up one of their own of the same kind, to depose English landlords and substitute Irish ones, to depose English monopoly of production and substitute Irish monopolists, will never give Ireland freedom. Until Irishmen, and Americans too, learn that not men but private property is the real source of oppression, both fair lands will be covered with poverty and ignorance—effects of oppression.

HAVE the people of the past been oppressed? Is the history of by-gone centuries that has come down to us but a pack of lies? Are all the bloody wars but myths? Are the stories of kings and nobles and untitled rich ruling in splendor over an impoverished working people but fiction? If there are any truths in history, or such events, could we not learn a lesson of great value by comparing the conditions now and then and see if there is any danger of history repeating itself? Are the social relations today and then anything alike? The masses of people today are too ignorant to make the comparison, have not even read the history of the past; but you, reader, are not of that class, I hope. You certainly have read some of the histories of olden time. In every land, in every age, land has been held as private property, bought and sold, as it is today. The owners of land had others till the soil, giving them food, clothing and shelter, or pay to get these things for their labor. It is just so today. Goods were bought and sold at a profit just as they are today. Money was loaned at interest just as it is today. Monopolies were operated just as they are today, only more limited in character. The rich oppressed the people by charging them for the use of the earth, for the use of money, for the exchange of goods, just as today. The rulers were called by various names and titles, but they made the laws just as today, and lived in splendor, raised armies and navies out of the taxes they laid upon the people, just as they do today. In command of the army, they either used it to kill and rob some weaker neighboring people, or to suppress any discontent in their own domain, just as is done today. In all these dark ages the working people were taught to be contented by men in the pay of the rulers just as they are today. They married, raised families, danced, picnicked, traded and schemed to cheat each other, just as they do today. They fawned before the rulers, hoping for favors above their fellows, just as the poor dupes fawn before the rich today. The poor then believed their condition was all they had a right to, that it was the only way things could be, that they could not possibly live except a king ruled over them, and that those who tried to show them a better way were enemies, just as the working people today believe they could not exist but for the rich to employ them and rule over them. The working people then would fight for the king against their own fellow workers, just as they do today at the command of a Pullman, Carnegie, Hill, Cleveland, or a judge. It is the same old play of kings under a new cloak. No king that ever lived had a revenue that would compare with the revenues of this land, and Croesus was a mendicant in comparison to the revenue taken from the working people today and here.

WHEN public work is let out by contract it revolves itself into this: The people collect from themselves a certain sum for a specified purpose and turn it over to some man or men to do the work, and place themselves at the mercy of this man or men, virtually saying to him: Pay us as little as you can get us to work for, and pocket the balance. They do not know enough to pay their own money to themselves for doing what they want done, and have no profit deducted to enrich some schemer.

ONE generation kills its reformers and the next makes heroes of them. Wendell Phillips and William Lloyd Garrison were anarchists and enemies of society forty years ago—today the apostles of liberty. Honest Old Abe was called a baboon thirty-five years ago. Today we know the greatness of his soul. Our Revolutionary fathers were rebels, traitors and enemies of the people—today they are deified. We cranks today can abide the time when our ideas will be accepted by the great people, embodied into law filling every family with peace, plenty and pleasure, and then we will be understood. It matters not if those active today shall have passed beyond, the world will be filled with joy and gladness because we did our duty in the best light we had. It is only a matter of a few revolutions of the earth when we go anyway and our lives may just as well be spent for providing juster conditions as anything else. To circulating literature, Oh, reformers, instead of to your tents, Oh, Israel.

WHAT a tale of misery and woe the advertisements unfold! One business man advertises the "bankrupt" stock of another fellow in ghoulish glee! Rejoicing over another's failure or business death because he will profit by it! Claims are joyfully made that the advertiser has bought the stock of some wretched tradesman at 25 cents on the dollar! Took four dollars' worth of property to enable some usurer to get his pound of flesh that called for one dollar! And if you say these statements are only to catch trade, then you have to admit the advertisers are liars, and if they are liars they are getting trade under false pretenses, and that means theft. Looked at in either way it is enough to make one heartsick. Oh, God! that people are so blind, so cruel, that they cannot see the horrors of a system prolific of so much misery and despair. Why, Oh, why will they vote to continue a system that makes life a burden, when one is offering at no cost that would make life a joy, a continually increasing pleasure?

If a hundred men, more or less, were wrecked on an island and should proceed to build one a palace and furnish him the best of everything, with servants to attend his wants, while the balance lived in shanties and had the coarsest food and clothing, would you not rightly pronounce the many fools? And would they be any less fools if it were a continent instead of an island and they were millions instead of a hundred? Change the law, make the monopolies public property and the rich will have to work for a living or starve. They will not get millions by bribing officers to give them franchises. So long as the law will recognize private property a few schemers and swindlers will have all the other people working like slaves for them.

A PASSING thought of what could be provided by public ownership of homes. Houses could be built cheaper, prettier and ten times more durable, with steel, glass and tiling, than they are at present. The cost of preparing for such work would be millions of dollars, but when once prepared, houses could be turned out like buttons, ready to be sewed on. Given the design, every piece of steel would come from the mill ready to be put in place—frame joists and rafters, cross-sections, etc. These could be made to receive glass panels of various designs and colors, the roof colored glass and the floors of tiling, and such a house would last for centuries, if the iron was protected from the weather. No dirt, no disease-breeding corners, no fire. The outside of the houses could be of panels of glass or marble or terra cotta. Such houses could be built, if enough were ordered, for less than the average wooden affair that rots down in twenty years. By having the public own them they could be provided for all, and at a cost far less than the tax on the average house today, for a rental.

As a large contractor can build houses with less days' labor than a small contractor could, so the hours of labor could be steadily decreased, better houses could be provided and all people furnished employment. No private employment will or can do this.